Commentaries on the Vedas, the Upanishads and the Bhagavad Gita

Commentaries on the Vedas, the Upanishads and the Bhagavad Gita

The Three Branches of India's Life-Tree

Sri Chinmoy

AUM PUBLICATIONS • NEW YORK

ISBN 0-88497-113-9

Aum Publications
86-10 Parsons Blvd.
Jamaica, NY 11432

You do not have to study the Vedas,
The Upanishads, the Mahabharata
And the Ramayana
To dive into the secret
And sacred wisdom-light
Of those scriptures.
He who realises God
Not only embodies all the scriptures—
Their essence and quintessence—
But also goes far, far beyond
The knowledge-seas of the past.

— *Sri Chinmoy*

CONTENTS

The Vedas: Immortality's First Call

The Upanishads: The Crown of India's Soul

Commentary on the Bhagavad Gita: The Song of the Transcendental Soul

INTRODUCTION

This volume brings together for the first time in English* Sri Chinmoy's commentaries on the Vedas, the Upanishads and the Bhagavad Gita, ancient Indian scriptures which are the foundation of the Hindu spiritual tradition. These talks were originally given at American universities and colleges in the early 1970s. Sri Chinmoy's approach is clear and practical, and at the same time searching and richly poetic. The book is both an excellent introduction for readers coming to this subject for the first time, and a series of illumining meditations for those who already know it well.

The Vedas

The Veda is a vast body of Sanskrit poetry, ritual treatises, dialogues and philosophical discourses which are the oldest surviving literature of India, and

*The collected commentaries have been previously published in a German translation: *Veden, Upanishaden, Bhagavadgita: Die drei Äste am Lebensbaum Indiens.* (Munich: Eugen Diederichs Verlag, 1994.)

among the oldest literature anywhere in the world. It was composed over a period of many centuries by inspired "seers" or rishis, probably (in the form we have now) beginning in the second millennium before our era. At the same time the Veda, or 'knowledge', is considered to have no date or human author, since the rishis did not invent but 'saw', in experiences of enlightenment, eternal truths which they transmitted in the form of sacred speech. The Veda is called 'the breath of the Supreme'. Its holy words embody the same Power as that which created the universe, for "the goddess Speech, the imperishable, is the first-form of Truth, mother of the Veda, the hub of Immortality."

The central religious practice of the Vedic people was the fire sacrifice, in which Agni, the fire god, was the intermediary between humans and the gods, great elemental yet also personal and spiritual forces of the cosmos. Agni is the sacrificial fire; he is in the sun and lightning and all the energies of nature—and he is that Light which emerged from the abyss of the Unmanifest at the very beginning of creation. Agni is also the mounting flame within the human heart which Sri Chinmoy calls 'aspiration': the inner cry to transcend ourselves. Seated before the outer, ceremonial fire, the Vedic seeker contemplated the presence of the divine and invoked Agni as his own inner light to open to him the world of the gods and the mysteries of sacred speech or *mantra,* which embodies in sound-form the fundamental realities of existence.

Over hundreds of years communion with the gods thus developed into an elaborate series of rituals with a fertile symbolic imagery. The hymns and incantations were sometimes devised as enigmas and might play with many levels of meaning. The symbol system of the Vedas became a key to the workings of the entire universe: visible nature, invisible realms, and the human mind, heart and soul. It was a language in which the seer-poets asked and answered the ultimate questions of life: What is the source of everything that we see and know? What is the secret of our own 'seeing' and 'knowing'? What is the basic pattern of all things? Who and what am I? As Sri Chinmoy has put it in this book:

> A philosopher is a poet in the mind.
> A poet is a philosopher in the heart.

The Upanishads

Their aspiration for understanding drew the Vedic sages at last to deep meditation on "That One", the supreme Brahman or the Person, God, Who existed before the gods themselves came into being. The teachings of the ancient seers of Truth, emerging from their spiritual realisation, are most succinctly expressed in the Upanishads, the final part of the Veda. In the words of Sarvepalli Radhakrishnan:

> The ideal which haunted the thinkers of the Upaniṣads, the ideal of man's ultimate beatitude, the perfection of knowledge, the vision of the Real in which the religious hunger of the mystic for divine vision and the philosopher's ceaseless quest for truth are both satisfied is still our ideal.*

The Upanishads have been the source for much of Indian philosophy, both traditional and modern, but their influence is no longer confined to India. Their brilliance and depths of intuition are always fresh, compelling and provocative. Their essential teaching is that the innermost self or soul of every living being is one with the divine. When one knows one's own true self or *atman,* one then also knows the highest reality and the ground of all existence. This realisation of oneness is the root of a universal love for all beings. It is reached by the practice of contemplative disciplines called *yoga* or 'union'. The aim of the yoga of the Upanishads is a total self-transformation culminating in God-knowledge and God-union: "He who knows Brahman becomes Brahman." As a modern seer-poet, a yogi and a knower of Brahman, Sri Chinmoy brings to his unique reflections on the meaning of the Upanishads his profound inner identification with their composers.

**The Principal Upaniṣads.* Edited and translated by S. Radhakrishnan. (New York: Humanities Press, 1953.)

The Bhagavad Gita and the Age of the Epics

As the Vedic age drew to its close in the middle of the first millennium BCE, a new civilization was taking shape in India, and with it a new Hindu scripture. The Vedas were not accessible to everyone. Their sheer size and complexity, as well as their ancient symbolic language and ritual technicalities, by this time made Vedic study the work of many years. The sages who held this tradition came to feel that a 'new Veda' was needed which would contain, in a form available to all, everything which was necessary for human life. From history and legend, from the devotions of the people, and from the Vedic revelation, two great epics were created: the Mahābhārata and the Rāmāyaṇa. Both are built around the lives of great heroes and saints and the war between good and evil. The Rāmāyaṇa tells of the deeds of Prince Rama of Ayodhya, for the Hindu faith one of the human Avatars, a 'descent' or incarnation of God. The Mahābhārata has as its core the story of five royal brothers, the Pāṇḍavas, and their rivalry with their cousins for the throne of the kingdom. They are helped in their struggles by Krishna, also a hero and a king, and another of the human Avatars. Both of the epics offer a vision of *dharma,* the right order of human life, along with teachings and abundant examples of how this vision can be manifested through right action.

The Mahābhārata contains the Bhagavad Gita or 'Song of the Lord', the teachings of Krishna given to his intimate friend and disciple Arjuna as the great battle climaxing the epic is about to begin. It is the best known of all Indian scriptures, and as Sri Chinmoy says, "the common property of all humanity." Countless seekers have found in the Gita not only inspiration and consolation, but also lucidly stated spiritual principles which they can apply in every inner and outer situation. Life is indeed a battle like the one Arjuna faces, and indeed Krishna teaches the way this battle can be faced, fought and won. Sri Chinmoy's commentary explains how and why. The teaching of the Bhagavad Gita is love, devotion and surrender, and the dynamic yoga of action which is possible only when we live in love. It is, in essence, Sri Chinmoy's own teaching as well—ancient, modern and eternal.

Only Sri Chinmoy could have written this book. On the strength of his own inner realisation, he is able to enter into these ancient Indian treasurehouses of spirituality, and also into the needs and aspirations of seekers of today. He achieves the communication to our present lives of truths first taught thousands of years ago, so that they can be understood, appreciated and used. He is fresh and powerful in expression, but also lyrical and soulful as only a spiritual Master who is also a poet can be. Even when he is at his most philosophically subtle or sublimely mystical, he never loses his compassionate connection with the immediate human concerns of the reader. One has only to read a sentence or two to recognise an unmistakable voice. One has only to read a page or two to find not only a great teacher but also a true friend.

KUSUMITA P. PEDERSEN

Jamaica, New York
1996

Note on Sanskrit transliteration:

In the interests of greater readability, for a few familiar names and terms the more popular spelling has been used instead of the standard Sanskrit transliteration with diacritical marks. These terms include the Rig and Sama Veda, Bhagavad Gita and Upanishad; Shankara, Chaitanya, Kali, Krishna, Rama, Shiva and Vishnu; Brahmin, Kshatriya, Vaishya and Shudra; rishi, maya and shakti.

Jyotishman Dam contributed the footnotes to the text.

The Vedas: Immortality's First Call

The Vedic Bird of Illumination

Dear sisters and brothers, I shall be giving seven talks on the Vedas at the Seven Sisters colleges. Interestingly, the Rig Veda itself deals with seven special sisters. It tells us that there is a divine chariot with only one wheel, and that this chariot is drawn by one horse with seven names. Seven sisters sing spiritual songs while standing before the chariot. While singing, the seven sisters reveal the concealed message of life's liberation and humanity's perfection (*Ṛgveda* I.164.3).

Seven is an occult number. In the spiritual world the number seven has a most special significance. In the hoary past there were seven great Indian sages who saw the Truth, lived the Truth and became the Truth.*

---

*The seven seers of the Rig Veda, called the *Āṅgirasaḥ* or 'human forefathers', were the spiritual fathers of humanity (according to Sri Aurobindo) and were later deified and worshipped. They first discovered the Light and "journeyed to the secret worlds of the shining felicity." Thus they would have been the great pioneers for all generations of spiritual seekers to come (cf. Sri Aurobindo, *The Secret of the Veda,*
(continued next page)

There are seven important rivers in India. A river signifies movement; water signifies consciousness. The movement of consciousness is a continuous progress towards the farthest Beyond.

There are seven notes in the musical scale. Each note has a special value of its own. Music is the mother tongue of humanity. God is the Supreme Musician. It is through music that we can enter into the universal harmony. It is through music that God's Beauty is being manifested in His all-loving creation.

There are seven colours in the rainbow. These colours indicate the stages of our spiritual journey toward the ultimate Goal. We all know that a rainbow is the sign of good luck and future progress. In the spiritual world, each colour of the rainbow is the harbinger of a new dawn.

There are seven higher worlds and seven lower worlds.* An aspiring human being enters into one of the seven higher worlds and makes progress in the inner life. Like a bird, his aspiring consciousness flies from one world to another, until finally he finds

---

Pondicherry, 1971, pp. 152ff. and 179ff.). In the Vedas they are invoked for the seekers' great journey towards Truth and Immortality. Even today they are offered oblations in India, like other ancestors.

*The Purāṇas, India's mythological scriptures, describe the seven underworlds *(Pātālas)* and the seven higher worlds (usually these are called *Bhū, Bhuva, Svar, Mahar, Jana, Tapas* and *Satya*). Our world *(Bhū)* is the lowest of the higher series.

himself in the seventh world, *Saccidānanda,* the world of Existence, Consciousness and Bliss. There he becomes consciously and inseparably one with the Supreme Pilot. But when a human being deliberately and knowingly does wrong things, heinous things, he is compelled to enter into one of the seven lower worlds, which are the worlds of darkness, bondage and ignorance.

Mother India is an aspiring tree. This aspiring tree has the Vedas as its only root. The root is Truth, the tree is Truth, the experience of the tree is Truth, the realisation of the tree is Truth, the revelation of the tree is Truth, the manifestation of the tree is Truth.

The Vedic seers saw the Truth with their souls, in their Heavenly visions and in their earthly actions.

> *Satyam eva jayate nānṛtam*
> *(Muṇḍakopaniṣad* 3.1.6*)*
>
> Truth alone triumphs, not falsehood.

This Truth teaches us how to be true brothers and sisters of humanity, conscious and devoted lovers of God and perfect masters of nature.

The Vedic teachings are universal. In the Yajur Veda we clearly observe that the teachings of the Vedas are for all—the Brahmins, the Kshatriyas, the Vaishyas, the Shudras, even the Chandalas, who are the degraded and the abandoned.* Men and women

*In later times Shudras, non-caste people and women were denied the study of the Vedas.

alike can study the Vedas. God is for all. The Vedas are for all. In the Vedic church no one is superior, no one is inferior; all are equal, all are children of God. These children of God can live in the heart of Truth and become the veritable pride of God.

Each Vedic seer is a poet and a prophet. In the case of an ordinary poet, his poems are quite often based upon imagination. Imagination gives birth to his poetry. In the case of the Vedic poets, it was intuition that gave birth to their poems. This intuition is the direct knowledge of Truth. As regards prophets, very often we see that an ordinary prophet's prophecy is based on a kind of unknown mystery. But in the case of the Vedic prophets, it was not so. Their prophecies were based on their full and conscious awareness of direct and immediate Truth. They brought to the fore this dynamic Truth to operate in the cosmic manifestation.

The present-day world believes that the mind can offer the highest possible experience of reality. The Vedic seers gave due importance to the mind, but they never considered the mind to be the source of the highest possible experience of reality.

The Vedas have the eternal wisdom. It is for us. The Vedas are more than willing to illumine us if we dare to listen to their message.

> *Śṛṇvantu viśve amṛtasya putrāḥ*
> (*Ṛgveda* X.13.1)
>
> Hearken, ye sons of Immortality.

This is their generous invitation.

When we live in the mind and do not want to go outside the boundaries of the mind, we remain bound in the trammels of the body. We remain in bondage. It is only the light from within and the guidance from Above that can liberate us from the teeming ignorance which has enveloped us. When we live in the mind, we live in the fabric of form. When we live in the soul, we enter into the formless and eventually go beyond both form and formlessness. We become, at that time, the individual soul universalised and the Universal Soul individualised.

The outer world is synonymous with the mind. The inner world is synonymous with the heart. The world of the eternal Beyond is synonymous with the soul. The outer world has the past, present and future. The inner world has the glowing and fulfilling future. The world of the Beyond has only the eternal Now. When we live in the outer world, the ignorant 'I' destroys us. When we live in the inner world, the illumined 'I' satisfies us. When we live in the world of the Beyond, the infinite 'I' fondly embodies us, reveals us and fulfils us. When we live in the mind, we cannot go beyond the judgment of destiny. Our human will is at the feet of destiny. When we live in the soul, we have free will. This free will is the Will of the Supreme. It is the will of the soul, which constantly identifies itself with the Will of the infinite Beyond.

Whether others believe it or not, the lovers of the Vedas know perfectly well that the Vedas are a significant contribution to the world of literature. These sublime literary scriptures are not just of national interest, for they offer international inspiration and universal aspiration. Just because they are international and universal, they fascinate and illumine sincere seekers in different countries at all times.

The Vedic mantras, or incantations, help us develop will-power in boundless measure. Even if we do not take the trouble of learning and repeating the mantras, we cultivate some will-power just by studying the Vedas devotedly. The paramount question is how we are going to use this will-power: to dominate the world or to serve God in the universe. If we live in the body for the pleasures of the body, we shall want to dominate the world. But if we live in the soul for the transformation and illumination of the body, then we shall serve God, love man and fulfil both God and man.

To say that the Vedas are badly infected with asceticism and other-worldliness is to betray one's own ignorance.* The Vedas are divinely practical and their message is of constant practical value. Needless to say, a great many Vedic seers were householders, and most of their pupils at the end of

---

*The widely-known Indian philosophy of asceticism and the concept of the world as an illusion, *māyā*, only found wide acceptance in much later times, beginning with Buddhism, and in Hinduism itself mainly with the great Vedantic philosopher Shankara (788-820 AD).

their instruction went home and became family men. The teachers in the seers taught their students the secret of eternal life and not the secret of unending death, which we learn from some of the destruction-loving teachers of science.

The Vedas do not embody depression, repression, self-mortification, sin-awareness or hell-consciousness. The Vedas embody the divine duty of the earthly life and the ever-increasing beauty of the Heavenly life. The Vedic seers accepted the heart of life to found the ultimate Reality upon earth. The Vedic seers accepted the body of death to carry it into the land of Immortality. Inspiration of the clear mind they liked. Aspiration of the pure heart they loved. Realisation of the sure soul they became.

Wellesley College
Wellesley, Massachusetts

The Glowing Consciousness of Vedic Truth

In Vedic times people lived with nature and played with intuition. The modern world lives with the mind's barren desert and plays with the body's frustration and the vital's destruction. In those days life was simple, and life's approach to the Goal was direct. Now man's life is complex, and man has two names: 'lifeless machine' and 'loud noise'.

Spontaneous intuition was the wisdom of the past. Constant suspicion is the wisdom of the present. In the Vedic age people knew the divine art of self-abnegation and self-dedication as today we know the human art of self-glorification and world-destruction. They cared for self-perfection first and then for world-perfection. We do not care for self-perfection at all; we care only for world-perfection. They were convinced that self-discipline would liberate them. We feel that self-discipline will limit us. They knew that self-discipline was not the end, but a means to the end, and that the end was *Ānanda*, Delight. We also know that self-discipline is not the end, but a means to the end. But for us, alas, the fatal end is self-destruction. The Vedic seers needed freedom. We also need freedom. To them, freedom was self-dedication to the life divine and the ever-transcending Beyond. To us, freedom is the imposition of our own reality-power on others.

There are four Vedas: the Rig Veda, the Sama Veda, the Yajur Veda and the Atharva Veda. The Rig Veda has 10,552 mantras. *Mantra* means 'incantation' or simply 'stanza'. The Sama Veda has 1,875 mantras, the Yajur Veda has 2,086 and the Atharva Veda has 5,987. A number of the Rig Vedic verses are also found in the other three Vedas. Most of the mantras in the Vedas are in the form of lucid poetry, except for some that are written in thought-invoking and rhythmic prose. The Vedas house the earliest poetry and prose literature of the searching, striving and aspiring human soul. He who thinks that the Vedic poetry is primitive and the Vedic literature insignificant is unmistakably wanting in mental illumination. How can primitive poetry offer such sublime and enduring wisdom to the world at large?

The body of the Vedic poetry is simplicity.
The vital of the Vedic poetry is sincerity.
The mind of the Vedic poetry is clarity.
The heart of the Vedic poetry is purity.
The soul of the Vedic poetry is luminosity.

There are two ways to study the Vedas. When we study the Vedas with the mind, we are constantly admonished by the strict vigilance of conscience. When we study the Vedas with the heart, we are unceasingly inspired by the flowing spontaneity of glowing consciousness.

The achievement of the mind is a scholar of the Vedas. The achievement of the heart is a lover of the Vedas. The scholar tries to satisfy the world without being satisfied himself. The lover feeds the world with the light of illumining manifestation and the delight of fulfilling perfection.

There are two words in the Vedas which are as important as the Vedas themselves. These two words are *satya* and *ṛta*, eternal Truth and eternal Law. Realisation and Truth embody each other. Manifestation and Law fulfil each other. If we do not live the Truth, we cannot reach the Goal. If we do not follow the Law, we cannot grow into the Goal.

The Vedic seers accepted the laws of others not only with their hearts' frankness but also with their souls' oneness. They saw the One in the many and the many in the One. To them, the Absolute was not their sole monopoly.

> *Satyam eva jayate nānṛtam*
> (*Muṇḍakopaniṣad* 3.1.6)
>
> Truth alone triumphs, not untruth.

Asato mā sad gamaya
Tamaso mā jyotir gamaya
Mṛtyor māmṛtaṃ gamaya
(*Bṛhadāraṇyakopaniṣad* 1.3.28)

Lead me from the unreal to the Real.
Lead me from darkness to Light.
Lead me from death to Immortality.

Unreality is untruth, and Reality is Truth. *Satya* is invoked by the pure heart. *Ṛta* is invoked by the brave vital. Love of Truth takes us from darkness. Love of divine order takes us from the human body to the divine life.

Radcliffe College
Cambridge, Massachusetts

The Inner Revelation-Fire

Why do we appreciate the teachings of the Vedas? We appreciate the teachings of the Vedas because they inspire us to rise and go beyond the body-consciousness. The Rig Veda inspires us to make the world great and perfect. The Sama Veda inspires us to become one with the divine melody and cosmic rhythm. The Yajur Veda tells us:

May our lives be successful
through self-sacrifice.
May our life-breath thrive
through self-sacrifice.

The Atharva Veda inspires us to go forward along the path of continuous progress. It tells us that Brihaspati, Guru of the cosmic gods, is leading and guiding us.

The Vedic seers saw fear in the outer world. They felt freedom in the inner world. They wanted to bring to the fore the freedom of the inner world through aspiration. In the Atharva Veda, the seers have offered us a significant prayer: "May we be fearless of those we know not and of those we know." (cf. *Atharvaveda, Paippalādasaṃhitā* III.35.5-6)

Fear of darkness is fear of the unknown.
Fear of Light is fear of the known.
Fear of the unknown is stupidity.
Fear of the known is absurdity.

What we need is the soul-will. Soul-will is God-freedom.

Uru ṇas tanve tan
Uru kṣayāya nas kṛdhi
Uru ṇo yaṃdhi jīvase (*Ṛgveda* VIII.68.12)

The Rig Veda's fiery utterance means: "Freedom for our body. Freedom for our home. Freedom for our life."

The Vedic way of life cannot be separated from ritual. In Vedic times, rituals were an integral part of life. In performing rituals seekers in the Vedic era made remarkable progress. In the Rig Veda, however, we see more emphasis on mental and inner philosophy than on ritual. This combination of ritual and philosophical wisdom is the wealth of the Vedic culture. Devotion and dedication loom large in ritual. Aspiration and meditation loom large in philosophical wisdom. In those days ritual disciplined and regulated life. Inner philosophy illumined and liberated life. In the heart of philosophy, the Light was discovered. In the body of ritual, the Light was manifested.

The Vedas specifically speak of three worlds: *pṛthivī*, the earth; *antarikṣa*, the sky; and *dyauḥ*, the celestial region.* On earth, matter is all. In the sky, divine activity is all. In Heaven, sentience is all.

Poetry and philosophy run abreast in the Vedas. Philosophy illumined the minds of the Vedic seers. Poetry immortalised their hearts. The philosopher is a poet in the mind. The poet is a philosopher in the heart. The philosopher likes outer religion and inner science. The poet likes outer art and inner literature. The philosopher says to the poet, "I give to you my precious wealth: wisdom, which is the constant and conscious instrument of intuition." The poet says to the philosopher, "I give to you my precious wealth: my devoted oneness with the life of light."

Many seers have seen the Truth, but when they reveal the Truth, quite often their revelations are not identical. What is really deplorable is that on different occasions, under different circumstances, their own revelations of the same Truth are found to be anything but identical. Here we must know that the differences exist only in the realisation and revelation of the Truth. There can be no difference in the Truth itself. Why do the differences occur? The differences occur because human individuality and personality do not see the Truth the way it has to be

---

*This is one of the well-known series of different worlds given in the Vedas, which represent gradations of the structure of the inner and outer universe.

seen. When the human personality and individuality are dissolved, the Truth remains one in realisation and one in revelation. Needless to say, the Vedas are the direct revelation of the seers' illumination, and not gifts from the unknown skies above.

There are people who think that the Vedas deal only with spirituality and not with science. They are mistaken. Advanced seekers and spiritual Masters are of the opinion that in the Yajur Veda there are many scientific truths which modern science has not yet discovered or acknowledged. The scientific knowledge of the Atharva Veda cannot be looked down upon either. The Vedic seers were aware of the process of cloud formation. They were fully aware of the different seasons. They knew the science of arithmetic and worked with figures in the millions, billions and trillions. In the Yajur Veda there is something even more striking. There we see evidence of the existence of airplanes. The Vedic seers used to make actual non-stop flights for hundreds of miles.* They also knew the secrets of geology, medicine and other sciences. All this, four thousand years ago!

The Vedas have been translated into many languages and admired and appreciated by many

---

**Yajurveda, Vājasaneyisaṃhitā* 17.59. Evidence of such airplanes *(vimāna)* is also to be found in other Vedic texts and above all in later books. See D.K. Kanjilal, *Vimana in Ancient India,* Calcutta, 1985.

foreigners. The great German philosopher Schopenhauer considered the Upanishads to be the consolation and illumination of his life.* We know that the Upanishads are the most powerful and most illumining children of the Vedas. But there is much truth in the saying that a translation cannot do full justice to the original. In the case of the Vedas, this is certainly true. Many people have translated the Vedas, but no matter how sincerely or devotedly they worked, a considerable amount of the Vedic beauty was lost.

There are four Vedas: the Rig Veda, the Yajur Veda, the Sama Veda and the Atharva Veda. The Rig Veda deals mainly with the forms of prayer. The Yajur Veda deals with sacrificial formulas. The Sama Veda deals with music. The Atharva Veda deals with medicine, science and magic formulas. In the Rig Veda the message of human evolution begins. The Rig Veda tells us the meaning of existence and of man's contribution to the world. The Yajur Veda teaches us how to perform the sacrifices correctly and how to control the universe. This Veda gives more importance to the mechanical side of sacrifices than to their spiritual aspect. The Sama Veda teaches us how divine music can elevate our aspiring consciousness into the highest realm of Bliss and make us conscious channels of God the Supreme Musician

---

*For the exact quote from Schopenhauer see page 43.

for the transformation of human darkness into divine light, human imperfection into divine perfection, human impossibilities into divine inevitabilities and human dreams into divine realities. The Atharva Veda teaches us how to control the spirits and lesser deities, and how to protect ourselves from evil spirits and destructive beings.

Vassar College
Poughkeepsie, New York

The Rig Veda

The Rig Veda is the oldest of all the Vedas. Most students of the Vedas are of the opinion that the Rig Veda is the most inspiring, most soulful and most fruitful Veda. This Veda embodies the earliest monument of India's aspiration and realisation. India's poetry, India's philosophy, India's literature, India's religion and India's science all owe their very existence to the Rig Veda, which was their source.

When it is a matter of choice between quality and quantity, the wise long for quality and the ignorant cry for quantity. The highest quality and the greatest quantity almost never go together. But to our great joy, the Rig Veda surpasses most strikingly the other three Vedas both in quantity and in quality. The Yajur Veda, the Sama Veda and the Atharva Veda have borrowed a considerable amount of wealth from the Rig Veda.

In the Rig Veda, the gods are seen as personifications of nature-power. The seers invoke the cosmic gods with their heart's prayers and their life's dedication. These gods were supposed to have been thirty-three in number. Each god had his own origin; all of them did not come into being at the same time. It is said that at first they accepted human incarnation and were mortals, as we are now. But by drinking *Soma*, Nectar, immortal they became. On the subtle physical plane, they are retaining the quintessence of their physical forms and earthly appearances. Some are warriors, while others are priests. Indra is the champion leader of the warriors, and Agni is the champion leader of the priests.

Power they have. Power they are. Some have the power of silence and peace, while others have the power of light and delight. Ceaselessly they fought against the formidable forces of evil, and eventually they did win the victory.

The Rig Vedic gods are kind and compassionate. With their boundless kindness and compassion, they fulfil the desires of the matter-loving world and the aspirations of the spirit-invoking life. They live in different homes: Heaven, air and earth. Heaven is the home of Vishnu, Varuṇa, Sūrya, Mitra and a few others.* The atmospheric region is for Indra, Rudra,

---

*Sri Chinmoy has said elsewhere (mainly in *The Dance of the Cosmic Gods,* New York, 1974) that these gods are personifications of these particular divine qualities: Vishnu, the Preserver, is the all-embracing consciousness and divine compassion. Indra is illumined, dynamic life-force. Agni is spiritual aspiration and inner will-power. Rudra is divine power and the fighter against ignorance, but at the same time compassion and peace. Sūrya is the light of illumination and liberation.

the Maruts and others. Agni and Bṛhaspati are well known among those who are considered to be terrestrial gods.

In the Rig Veda we see the pure presence of devotion and the sure presence of knowledge. Devotion tells us how sweet and compassionate God is. Knowledge tells us how high and great God is. Devotion and knowledge find their complete satisfaction only in service. Service is concentration. Devotion is prayer. Knowledge is meditation. Only concentrated service, devoted prayer and illumined meditation can make us divinely great and supremely perfect.

According to the Vedas, action is a most essential part of life. Action is the conscious acceptance of our earthly existence. Action needs the body, which is its temple and fortress. Action needs life, which is its inspiration and aspiration. A man of action is an ideal hero in the battlefield of life. He lives with God's human body, the earth, and works for God's divine life, Heaven. Action is outer sacrifice and inner oneness. The Rig Veda offers us a supreme secret as to what kind of sacrifice we can make on the strength of our oneness. In action we see the universal presence of God. In action we embody the spirit and reveal the form. In the spirit is God the Absolute. In the form is God the Infinite.

The Rig Veda speaks of God the Power:

Tvam Indra balād adhi sahaso jāta ojasaḥ …
(*Ṛgveda* X.153.2)

O God, Thy existence rests on strength, valour and energy.
O Mighty One, You are Strength itself.

In order to manifest God considerably on earth, the seeker must live a long life.

Aum bhadraṃ karṇebhiḥ śṛṇuyāma devāh …*
(*Ṛgveda* I.89.8)

O cosmic gods, may we hear with our ears what is good and auspicious.
May we see with our eyes what is good and auspicious.

But merely living a long life lacking in divinity is nothing short of stark ignorance.

The seers of the Rig Veda regard God as the eternal Father, Mother and Friend. They also feel that God is their Beloved. God has many aspects, but a devoted seer prefers the aspect of God as Lord. He prays to his Lord for Compassion and Benediction. He has come to realise that if he has God's Love and God the Love, then he needs nothing else from either earth or Heaven.

---

*Sri Chinmoy usually writes *'Aum'* instead of *'Om'* because in Sanskrit 'o' is a diphthong formed by 'a' and 'u', thus stressing the triple aspect of *'Aum'*. See also the author's summary of the contents of the Māṇḍūkya Upanishad on page 44.

The Rig Vedic seers are the teachers of mankind. The Rig Vedic gods are the saviours of mankind. The teachers are teaching the world the message of Light and Truth. The saviours are healing the unaspiring, blind and deaf world, and championing the genuine seekers. The Rig Vedic seers are the builders of Hindu culture and Hindu civilisation. They represent the dawn of Hindu inspiration and the noon of Hindu aspiration. They offer to the world at large the ultimate meaning of religion. According to them, religion is the inner code of life. In each religion is a love-branch of the Truth-Tree. The Rig Vedic gods tell us to accept life with love, enjoy life with renunciation and fulfil life with surrender to the Will of the Absolute.

The Vedas tell us that we are cattle of the gods. Unfortunately, we are now compelled to feel that we are slaves of the machine. Let us aspire. Our aspiration will once more make us cattle of the gods. Later, our realisation will make us lambs of the gods. Finally, our manifestation will make us lions of the Absolute Supreme.

Aspiration we have. Realisation we need. Manifestation God and we together need.

Barnard College
New York, New York

The Song of the Infinite

The Vedas are the most ancient scriptures in the library of consciously evolving humanity. For our own conscious evolution we may be inspired to read the Vedas by Max Müller's encouragement: "I maintain that for everybody who cares for himself, for his ancestors, for his history, for his intellectual development, a study of Vedic literature is indispensable."*

The Vedas embody intuitive visions, divine experiences and life-illumining realities. From the ignorance-sea we have to enter into the knowledge-sea. The Rig Veda inspires us, saying, "The vessels of Truth carry men of good deeds across the ocean of ignorance." (*Ṛgveda* IX.73.1)

Present-day human life is nothing but an endless despondency. To come out of the trap of despondency is almost impossible. The Yajur Veda offers us

---

*Friedrich Max Müller (1823 – 1900) was perhaps the greatest German indologist of the 19th century. He was professor of linguistics at Oxford and distinguished himself by translating and editing the Rig Veda as well as editing the series *Sacred Books of the East*.

a solution: "He who sees all existence in the Self and the Self in all existence, falls not into the trap of blighting and weakening despondency."

The Vedas are universal; hence, the West can claim them as well as the East. The great American philosopher Thoreau said something most significant about the Vedas: "What extracts from the Vedas I have read fall on me like the light of a higher and purer luminary which describes a loftier course through purer stratum, free from particulars, simple, universal. The Vedas contain a sensible account of God." Undoubtedly they do.

The firm belief of Sir William Jones is challenging and at the same time illumining: "I can venture to affirm, without meaning to pluck a leaf from the never-fading laurels of our immortal Newton, that the whole of his theology, and part of his philosophy, may be found in the Vedas."

The Vedic commandment for the human physical is *śaucam*. *Śaucam* means 'purity'—purity in the body and purity of the body. Without the body's purity, nothing divine in us can expand; nothing divine in us can be permanent.

The Vedic commandment for the human vital is *ahiṃsā*. *Ahiṃsā* means 'non-violence'—non-violence in the vital and non-violence of the vital. It is from non-violence that man gets his greatest opportunity to feel that he does not belong to a small family, but to the largest family of all: the universe. India's philosophy of non-violence was first put into practice by the compassionate Lord Buddha and his followers, and by the Lord Mahāvir and the followers of Jainism. Gandhi's non-violence was a most precious gift to the life-loving humanity of the present.

The Vedic commandment for the human mind is *satyam. Satyam* means 'truth' or 'truthfulness'. Truthfulness in the mind and truthfulness of the mind alone can lead us to a higher life, a life of illumining Divinity and fulfilling Immortality.

The Vedic commandment for the human heart is *Īśvarapraṇidhāna. Īśvarapraṇidhāna* means the heart's loving devotion to the Lord Supreme. When we have pure and spontaneous devotion for the Supreme Lord, we feel our inseparable oneness with Him, with the Eternity of His Spirit, with the Infinity of His Body and with the Immortality of His Life.

In the Vedas the concept of sacrifice looms very large. We sacrifice to God what we have: ignorance. God sacrifices to us what He is: Perfection. God's sacrifice is always unconditional. Our sacrifice at times is conditional and at times is unconditional. In conditional sacrifice we fight and win the battle. In unconditional sacrifice we do not have to fight at all, for the victory is already won. Victory is our birthright; it is forever ours.

Sacrifice is self-offering. Self-offering is self-fulfilment. Self-fulfilment is love-manifestation and

Truth-perfection. Through our outer sacrifice we become a divine part of Mother-Earth. Through our inner sacrifice we become an immortal part of Father-Heaven. We make the outer sacrifice when we come out of the domain of binding desires and enter into the domain of liberating aspiration. We make the inner sacrifice when we try to manifest God in the world of ignorance after having achieved God-realisation. The outer sacrifice demands the strength of a hero. The inner sacrifice demands the power of an army. With our outer sacrifice we see the Truth. With our inner sacrifice we become the Truth.

Mount Holyoke College
South Hadley, Massachusetts

Intuition-Light from the Vedas

Scholars as well as students disagree over the origin of the Vedas. I find this controversy foolish. The Vedas are as old as the conscious aspiration of the universe. But the universe is consciously or unconsciously evolving into perfection, whereas the Vedas contain the beginning of inspiring perfection and the end of illumining realisation.

When we say that the Vedas are eternal, we do not mean that the four scriptures have no beginning and no end. What we mean is that the real meaning of the Vedas, which is the knowledge of God, has neither beginning nor end. The Vedas are the direct experiences and revelations of the rishis of the hoary past. These experiences may be had by any sincere seeker of the Truth, at any time and in any place.

Unlike other scriptures, the Vedas have the sincere and brave heart to say that they are not indispensable; nay, not even important. They say that what is really important and supremely indispensable is the realisation of Brahman, the One without a second. Nevertheless, if we want to study the Vedas, we have to study with the help of an illumined teacher. The Vedas themselves instruct the seeker to approach a Teacher. They also say that the Teacher has to be approached with a heart of humility and a life of dedicated service.

Karma, which means 'work' or 'service', and *jñāna*, or knowledge, are the principal teachings of the Vedas. Through *jñāna* we realise the absolute Truth, and through *karma* we manifest our realisation.

According to the Vedas there are four important stages in life: student-life, marriage-life, retirement-life and renunciation-life. Student-life is self-discipline. Marriage-life is self-control and self-regulation. Retirement-life is peace and tranquility. Renunciation-life is the offering of what one has and what one is to the Absolute Supreme.

> *Ekaṃ sad viprā bahudhā vadanti*
> (*Ṛgveda* I.164.46)
>
> Truth-existence is one.
> Sages call it by various names.

This Truth-existence is experienced and realised in different ways by each seeker of the infinite Truth according to his own inner development. Just because of this lofty message from the Vedas, India's religious heart is large and cosmopolitan. India's spiritual heart knows how to accept other religions, how to appreciate other religions and how to admire other religions. India's spiritual heart has realised that for each new religion there is a new approach to the Goal. Each path is right and indispensable for its own followers.

In order to realise the highest Truth we need three things: inspiration, aspiration and intuition. Inspiration asks us to run toward the Goal. Aspiration asks us to fly toward the Goal. Intuition asks us to see and feel the Truth directly, and to grow into the very essence of Truth.

The word *saramā* symbolises intuition. *Saramā* is the hound of Heaven who enters into the world of inconscience and discovers its concealed treasures: light and delight. *Saramā* is the dawn of Truth in a dedicated body, dynamic vital and aspiring heart. *Saramā* and the straight path go together. *Saramā* follows the straight and sunlit path and arrives at the Truth. The path of fear and doubt, error and terror, *Saramā* never follows. *Saramā* secretly and cautiously enters into the heart of illumination, and openly and bravely walks in the life of revelation, so that the hostile forces cannot thwart or destroy her progress. So that the Truth-consciousness can be realised as a whole by all seekers, *Saramā* travels between earth's cry and Heaven's smile. *Saramā* is the seeker who seeks Truth-consciousness. *Saramā* is the lover who loves earth's conscious ascent and Heaven's illumining descent. *Saramā* is the player who plays with the seer's vision in the inner world and plays hide-and-seek with the beginner's inspiration in the outer world.

The Vedas: Immortality's First Call

The Vedas are at once the sky of Light and the sea of Delight. The Light-sky is the vastness of Truth. The Delight-sea is the immensity of Truth. Light and Delight are perpetual runners. Sometimes Light precedes Delight. Sometimes Delight precedes Light. When Light touches the earth-consciousness, earth is divinely transformed. When Delight touches the earth-consciousness, earth is supremely fulfilled.

Light is the birth of God.
Delight is the life of God.
Light is the smile of universal oneness.
Delight is the smile of transcendental perfection.
Light is what God has.
Delight is what God is.

Smith College
Northampton, Massachusetts

The Wisdom-Sun of Vedic Truth

When we study the Vedas, we should be aware of two different things: the esoteric interpretations of the Vedas made by illumined spiritual Masters and the mental conclusions made by scholars and historians. Each esoteric interpretation by a Master is founded upon a direct intuitive vision of the Truth, whereas each mental conclusion of a scholar or historian is founded upon unillumined mental analysis and hesitant, uncertain research.

The seers of the hoary past saw the Truth and revealed the Truth. Seekers of all ages feel the Truth and use the Truth. But most scholars do not care for the realisation of the Truth; they care only for the manifestation of the Truth. They care more for the form than for the spirit of the Vedas. Most historians put the lesser truths mentioned in the Vedas, those relating to the caste system and magic formulas, in the vanguard of their discussions, and pay little attention to the highest Truth, the knowledge of Brahman. They have no time to know soulfully and devotedly the life-energising and life-fulfilling messages that the Vedas actually contain. The life-giving and life-revealing messages of the Vedas do not seem to interest them. The birth of the Vedas, the outer growth of the Vedas and the decline of the Vedic influence on India are more than enough to satisfy them.

The Vedas are meant for the lovers of eternal Time, not for the lovers of fleeting earthly time. The Vedas are meant for those who love God the Truth, and not for those who love merely the body of obscure history, which embodies the life of complication and confusion.

Professor Max Müller undoubtedly loved India. He wrote considerably on Indian scriptures. But those who feel that Max Müller's love for India had a secret motive are perfectly correct. In utmost secrecy, in the inmost recesses of his heart it seems that he wanted to convert India—the Indian mind and the Indian heart—to Christianity. For example, he wrote to the Secretary of State for India, the Duke of Argyl, in 1868:

> The ancient religion of India is doomed, and if Christianity does not step in, whose fault will it be?

And to his wife in 1886, he wrote:

> I hope I shall finish the work, and I feel convinced, though I shall not live to see it, that this edition of mine and the translation

> of the Vedas will hereafter tell to a great extent on the fate of India and on the growth of millions of souls in that country. It is the root of the religion, and to show them what the root is, I feel sure, is the only way of uprooting all that has sprung from it during the last 3,000 years.

When he extolled India to the skies, he was sincere in his praise. It came from the depths of his heart. But his desire to convert India to Christianity was equally sincere. That feeling too, I am sure, came from the depths of his heart. His was a life of complexity.

Had Max Müller not studied the Upanishads, had he not been illumined by the light of the Upanishads, he would not have been acclaimed by the entire world. His name would have remained unknown in the world's literature. If it is true that he brought the Upanishads to the world at large, then it is equally true that the touch of the Upanishadic light brought him fame.

The Vedas and the Vedic hymns are inseparable. Each hymn is an invocation to a particular god or deity. Each hymn is a discovery of a *kavi*, *rishi* or *vipra*—a Vedic poet, a Vedic seer or a Vedic sage. Each Vedic discovery is a boon from God. Each boon is a spark of light. Each spark of light is an accomplishment of God in man and an accomplishment of man in God. Man's ultimate accomplishment is the transformation of human nature. God's ultimate accomplishment is the perfection of the earth-consciousness.

Life is an idea; life is an ideal. Life has a soul; life has a goal. The Vedic idea of life is the idea of Truth. The Vedic ideal of life is the ideal of Bliss. The Vedic soul is the soul of multiplicity in unity. The Vedic goal is the goal of unifying earth's wideness and Heaven's abundance.

India had the Vedic seers of Truth. India has seekers of Truth. The supreme task of the seers was to bring the cosmic gods and deities down into the earth-consciousness. They performed their task. Now it is the task of the seekers to keep the gods and deities here on earth and help them in their cosmic play. The Supreme saw His infinite potentialities and possibilities in the seers. The Supreme sees His manifesting Reality and fulfilling Perfection in the seekers.

Bryn Mawr College
Bryn Mawr, Pennsylvania

The Upanishads: The Crown of India's Soul

India's Soul-Offering

India's soul-offering is the perennial light of the Upanishads. The Upanishads offer to the world at large the supreme achievement of the awakened and illumined Hindu life.

The Vedas represent the cow. The Upanishads represent milk. We need the cow to give us milk, and we need milk to nourish us.

The Upanishads are also called the Vedānta. The literal meaning of Vedānta is 'the end of the Vedas.' But the spiritual meaning of Vedānta is 'the cream of the Vedas, the pick of the inner lore, the aim, the goal of the inner life.' The Muktika Upanishad tells us something quite significant:

> *Tileṣu tailavad vede vedāntaḥ supratiṣṭhitaḥ*
> (*Muktikopaniṣad* 1.1.9)

> Like oil in the sesame seed, Vedānta is established essentially in every part of the Vedas.

The Upanishads tell us that there are two types of knowledge: a higher knowledge and a lower knowledge. *Paravidyā* is the higher knowledge, and *aparavidyā* is the lower knowledge. The higher knowledge is the discovery of the soul. The lower knowledge is the fulfilment of the body's countless demands.

According to our Indian tradition, there were once 1,180 Upanishads. Each came from one branch, or *śākhā*, of the Vedas. Out of these, two hundred Upanishads made their proper appearance, and out of these two hundred, one hundred and eight Upanishads are now traceable. If a seeker wants to get a glimpse of truth, light, peace and bliss, then he must assiduously study these one hundred and eight Upanishads. If a real seeker, a genuine seeker, wants to get abundant light from the Upanishads, then he has to study the thirteen principal Upanishads. If he studies the principal Upanishads, and at the same time wants to live the Truth that these Upanishads embody, then he will be able to see the face of Divinity and the heart of Reality.

The thirteen principal Upanishads are *Īśā, Kaṭha, Kena, Praśna, Muṇḍaka, Māṇḍūkya, Chāndogya, Bṛhadāraṇyaka, Taittirīya, Aitareya, Śvetāśvatara, Kaivalya* and *Maitrī.*

> *Tad ejati tan naijati tad dūre tadvantike …*
> (*Īśopaniṣad* 5)
>
> That moves, and That moves not.
> That is far, and the same is near.
> That is within all this.
> That is also without all this.

The Īśā Upanishad has this special message for us. To the desiring mind, this message is vapid, nebulous, puzzling and confusing. To the aspiring heart, this message is inspiring and illumining. To the revealing soul, this message is fulfilling and immortalising. Brahman, God, in His Absolute aspect, is immutable; but in His conditioned aspect He is ever-changing, ever-transforming, ever-evolving, ever-revealing, ever-manifesting and ever-fulfilling.

Again, the Īśā Upanishad reconciles work and knowledge, the One and the many, the impersonal God and the personal God, in a striking manner. Work done with detachment is real knowledge. When we consciously try to see God in everything and in everybody, we soulfully offer ourselves to dedicated action. Thus knowledge is action. The One and the many: we need the One for our self-realisation; we need the many for our self-manifestation. The impersonal God and the personal God: when we live in the impersonal God, we see Truth in its illumining vision. When we live in the personal God, we see Truth in its revealing reality.

The Son of God declared, "I and my Father are one." (John 10:30) The Chāndogya Upanishad makes a bold statement, to some extent more daring and at the same time more convincing:

> *Tat twam asi*
> (*Chāndogyopaniṣad* VI.8.7–VI.16 passim)
>
> That thou art.

What does it mean? It means that you are none other than God. Who else is God, if not you?

A God-lover knocked at God's Heart-Door. God, from within, said, "Who is it?"

The God-lover said, "It is I." The door remained locked. The man knocked and knocked. Finally he went away.

After an hour he came back, and again he knocked at God's Heart-Door. God, from within, said, "Who is it?"

The God-lover said, "It is I." The door remained locked. The man knocked and knocked at the door in vain. Finally he left.

After another hour, again he came back and knocked at God's Heart-Door. From within, God said, "Who is it?"

The God-lover said, "My Eternal Beloved, it is Thou." God immediately opened His Heart-Door.

When a seeker feels this kind of intimate and inseparable oneness with God, God opens His Heart-Door to him and offers him His very Throne.

The Upanishadic seers felt no necessity to go to any spiritual centre, no necessity to go to a temple, no necessity to hear a talk or a sermon or even to study books. God was their only outer book, and God was their only inner teacher. God-realisation was their only necessity, and God-manifestation was their only reality.

The great German philosopher Schopenhauer voiced forth, "In the whole world there is no study so beneficial and so elevating as that of the Upanishads. It has been the solace of my life; it will be the solace of my death. They are the products of the highest wisdom."*

The Upanishads offer us three lessons. The first lesson is *Brahman.* The second lesson is *ātman.* The third lesson is *jagat. Brahman* is God, *ātman* is the soul and *jagat* is the world. When we meditate on Brahman, our life grows into immortalising Bliss. When we meditate on the soul, our life becomes a conscious and speedy evolution. When we do not neglect the world, our life becomes fulfilling manifestation.

If you study the Upanishads, not in a cursory or perfunctory manner, but with the mind's clarity, then you will see that God and you, you and God, are eternal. If you study the Upanishads with your heart's receptivity, you will see that God and you are equal. Finally, if you study the Upanishads with your soul's light, you will come to realise that there in Heaven you are the realised and esoteric God, and here on earth you are the manifested and exoteric God.

> *Nāyam ātmā balahīnena labhyo*
> (*Muṇḍakopaniṣad* 3.2.4)
>
> The soul cannot be won by the weakling.

---

*Arthur Schopenhauer, *Parerga und Paralipomena II,* 184 and 185.

The inner strength dethrones the idol which has been installed by fear and doubt. When your inner strength comes to the fore, the doubter in you will be transformed into the soul's effulgent light.

The Upanishads are the obverse of the coin of which the reverse is consciousness. There are three states of ordinary consciousness: *jāgṛti*, *svapna* and *suṣupti*. *Jāgṛti* is the waking state, *svapna* is the dreaming state, *suṣupti* is the state of deep sleep. There is another state of consciousness which is called *turīya*, the pure consciousness of the Transcendental Beyond.

The Māṇḍūkya Upanishad offers us a most significant gift. It tells us about the Universal Soul. The Universal Soul has two aspects: *vaiśvānara* and *virāṭ*. The microcosmic aspect is called *vaiśvānara*; the macrocosmic aspect is called *virāṭ*. *Jāgṛti*, the waking state; *vaiśvānara*, the physical condition; and the letter 'A' from Aum, the sound symbol of *Prakṛti,* the primal energy, form the first part of Reality. *Svapna*, the dreaming state; *taijasa*, the brilliant intellectual impressions; and 'U' from Aum form the second part of Reality. *Suṣupti*, the state of deep sleep; *prājña*, the intuitive knowledge; and 'M' from Aum form the third part of Reality.

Turīya, the fourth state of consciousness, at once embodies and transcends these three states of consciousness. On the one hand, it is one part of the four parts; on the other hand, it is the culminating whole, the end, the Goal itself. *Turīya* is the Reality eternal, beyond all phenomena. *Turīya* is the Transcendental Brahman. *Turīya* is *Saccidānanda*—Existence, Consciousness, Delight. It is here, in *turīya*, that a highly advanced seeker or a spiritual Master can actually hear the soundless sound, Aum, the supreme secret of the Creator.

The supreme wealth of the Upanishads is the Self:

> *Yato vāco nivartante aprāpya manasā saha ...*
> (*Taittirīyopaniṣad* II.4 and II.9)

> Whence the words, the power of speech come back with the mind baffled, the goal unattained.

This Self cannot be won by mental brilliance. It can be won only with an aspiring heart and a dedicated life.

This Transcendental Self is covered here in the world of relativity by five distinct sheaths: *annamaya kośa*, the gross physical sheath; *prāṇamaya kośa*, the sheath of the vital force; *manomaya kośa*, the mental sheath; *vijñānamaya kośa*, the sheath of the advanced and developed knowledge; and *ānandamaya kośa*, the sheath of Bliss.

There are three types of bodies corresponding to these five sheaths. These bodies are called *sthūlaśarīra*, *sūkṣmaśarīra* and *kāraṇaśarīra*. *Sthūla* means 'gross physical', and *śarīra* means 'body'. *Sūkṣma* means 'subtle', and *kāraṇa* means 'causal'. The physical body, *sthūlaśarīra,* comprises *annamaya kośa,* the material substance. *Sūkṣmaśarīra,* the subtle body, comprises *prāṇamaya kośa, manomaya kośa* and *vijñānamaya kośa. Kāraṇaśarīra,* the causal body, comprises *ānandamaya kośa*, the sheath of Bliss.*

On a dark and tenebrous night the glow-worms appear. They offer their light and feel that it is they who have chased the darkness away. After a while the stars start shining, and the glow-worms realise their insufficient capacity. After some time the moon appears. When the moon appears, the stars see and feel how dim and insignificant their light is in comparison to the light of the moon. In a few hours the sun appears. When the sun appears, the joy and pride of the moon are also smashed. The sunlight chases away all darkness, and the light of the glow-worms, stars and moon pales into insignificance.

This is the outer sun. But each of us has an inner sun. This inner sun is infinitely more powerful, more beautiful, more illumining than the outer sun. When this sun shines, it destroys the darkness of millennia. This sun shines through Eternity. This inner sun is called the Self, the Transcendental Self.

Princeton University
Princeton, New Jersey

---

*This is taught in *Taittirīyopaniṣad* II.2–5.

The Revelation of India's Light

Each Upanishad is the unfoldment of the supreme knowledge which, once spiritually attained, is never lost. According to the Upanishads, the entire universe of action, with its ephemeral means and ends, lives in the meshes of ignorance. It is the knowledge of the supreme Self that can destroy the human ignorance of millennia and inundate the earth-consciousness with the Light and Delight of the ever-transcending and ever-manifesting Beyond.

As we have the heart, the mind, the vital, the body and the soul, so also the Upanishads have a heart, a mind, a vital, a body and a soul. The heart of the Upanishads is self-realisation, the mind of the Upanishads is self-revelation, the vital of the Upanishads is self-manifestation, the body of the Upanishads is self-transformation and the soul of the Upanishads is self-perfection.

What is of paramount importance right now is self-realisation. For self-realisation we need only four things. First we need the help of the scriptures, then a spiritual guide, then yogic disciplines and finally the Grace of God. The scriptures tell the seeker,

"Awake, arise! It is high time for you to get up! Sleep no more!" The spiritual Master tells the seeker, "My child, run! Run the fastest! I am inspiring you. I have already kindled the flame of aspiration within you. Now you can run the fastest." Yogic disciplines tell the seeker, "You are practising the spiritual life, and I am giving you the result of your practice. I have made the road clear for you. Now you can run the fastest on a road that is empty of danger." Then something more is required, and that is God's Grace. One may run the fastest, but one may not reach the Goal even if there is no obstacle on the way, because human beings very often get tired. Before they reach the Goal, they feel that they are totally exhausted. At that time what is required is God's Grace. Without God's Grace one cannot complete the journey. God's Grace tells the seeker, "Lo, the Goal is won."

To be sure, God's Grace starts right from the beginning. When we study the scriptures, God's Grace has already dawned on us. Had there been no Grace from God, we could not have stepped onto the spiritual path in the first place. And had there been no Grace from God, we could not have found our spiritual Master. It is out of His infinite Bounty that God brings a seeker to the Master. Then the seeker and the Master must play their respective roles. The Master will bring down God's Compassion, but the seeker has to practise spiritual disciplines. His task is to aspire, and the Master's task is to bring down Compassion.

In the inner life, one thing that everybody must have is aspiration. Here on earth the tree offers us an example of this aspiration. It remains on earth with its roots in the dirt, but its aim is to reach the Highest. We are afraid of staying on earth. We feel that if we stay on earth, we cannot reach the Highest. But the tree shows us how absurd this is. Its roots are under the ground, but its topmost branch is aspiring towards the heavens. In the Upanishads we come across a tree called the *aśvattha* tree. Unlike earthly trees, this tree has its roots above and its branches below. It has two types of branches. One type enters into the meshes of ignorance and then starts struggling, fighting and trying to come out again into the effulgence of Light. The other type of branch always tries to remain in the Light. Its movement is upward; its aspiration is upward.

Here on earth each human being has capacity. A human being sees ignorance within and without, but he has the capacity to remain beyond the boundaries of ignorance. How? Through aspiration. Why? Because he needs constant satisfaction. And it is aspiration alone that can give us this constant satisfaction. Why do we aspire? We aspire for Delight, *Ānanda*. Delight is self-creation and self-experience. Delight in the Highest, absolute Highest, is known as *Ānandapuruṣa*. There the Delight is Infinity, Eternity and Immortality. There is another type of Delight which is called *ānandātmā,* when from infinite Delight, Delight takes shape and form. In the earth-bound consciousness, Delight is called *ānandātmā.*

When Delight gradually descends into the obscure, impure, unlit, imperfect nature of man to transform human nature, it finds constant resistance. Then we see that Delight loses its power because of teeming ignorance and pleasure, short-lived pleasure, looms large. In the Highest, the triple consciousness—*Saccidānanda*—Existence, Consciousness and Delight go together. But when they want to manifest themselves, they have to do it only through Delight.

When Delight descends, the first rung that it steps on is called the Supermind. The Supermind is not something a little superior to the mind. No, it is infinitely higher than the mind. It is not 'mind' at all, although the word is used. It is the consciousness that has already transcended the limitations of the finite. There creation starts. One rung below is the Overmind. Here multiplicity starts in an individual form. The next rung is the intuitive mind. With the intuitive mind we see multiplicity in a creative form. With intuition we see all at a glance. We can see many things at a time; we see collective form. From the intuitive mind, Delight enters into the mind proper. This mind sees each object separately. But although it sees everything separately, it does not try to doubt the existence of each object. Next, Delight enters into the physical mind—that is, the mind that is governed by the physical. This mind sees each object separately, plus it doubts the existence of each object. Real doubt starts in the physical mind.

After it has descended through all the levels of the mind, Delight enters into the vital. In the vital we see the dynamic force or the aggressive force. The force that we see in the inner or subtle vital is dynamic, and the force that we see in the outer vital is aggressive. From the vital, Delight enters into the physical. There are two types of physical: the subtle physical and the physical proper. In the subtle physical, Delight is still descending, and we may still be conscious of it. But in the subtle physical we cannot possess or utilise the Truth; we can only see it, like a beggar looking at a multi-millionaire. Finally, when we come to the gross physical, there is no Delight at all.

Delight descends, but we do not see even an iota of it in the gross physical. What can we do then? We can enter into the soul on the strength of our aspiration, and the soul will consciously take us to the highest plane, to *Saccidānanda*—Existence, Consciousness, Bliss. At that time our journey can become conscious. We have entered into the triple consciousness, and we can begin descending consciously into the Supermind, the Overmind, the intuitive mind, the mind proper, the physical mind, the vital and the physical. When we are successful in the physical, when we can bring down Delight from the highest plane and the physical can absorb and utilise this Delight, the life of pleasure ends. At that time we come to realise the difference between the life of pleasure and the life of Delight. The life of pleasure is followed by frustration and destruction. The life of Delight is a continuous growth, continuous fulfilment, continuous achievement and continuous God-manifestation in God's own Way.

The Muṇḍaka Upanishad (*Muṇḍakopaniṣad* 3.1.1-2) has offered us two birds. One bird is seated on the top of the life-tree, the other on a branch below. The bird seated on the low branch eats both sweet and bitter fruits. Sweet fruits give the bird the feeling that life is pleasure; bitter fruits give the bird the feeling that life is misery. The other bird, seated on the top of the tree, eats neither the sweet fruit nor the bitter fruit. It just sits calmly and serenely. Its life is flooded with peace, light and delight. The bird that eats the sweet and bitter fruit on the tree of life is disappointed and disgusted; disappointed because pleasure is impermanent, ephemeral and fleeting; disgusted because frustration ends in destruction. Unmistakably disappointed and utterly disgusted, this bird flies up and loses itself in the freedom-light and perfection-delight of the bird at the top of the life-tree. The bird on the top of the tree is the Cosmic and Transcendental Self, and the bird below is the individual self. These two beautiful birds are known as *Suparṇā.*

In some of the Upanishads we see a continuous rivalry between the gods and the demons. The self-resplendent ones are the gods; and the self-indulgent ones are the demons. The gods and the demons are the descendents of Prajāpati, the Creator. When the gods win the victory, the light of the soul reigns supreme. When the demons win the victory, the night of the body reigns supreme. Originally the gods and the demons were the organs of Prajāpati. The organs that were energised by the divine Will, illumined by the divine Light and inspired by the divine Action became gods. The organs that were instigated by the lower thoughts, were eager to live in the sense-world and enjoy pleasure-life, and were aiming at lesser and destructive goals, became demons. Needless to say, it is infinitely easier to reach the lesser goals than it is to reach the Goal Supreme. This is precisely why the demons greatly outnumbered the gods. But we, the seekers of the infinite Light and Truth, need the quality of the gods, not the quantity of the demons.

Once the gods made a fervent request to the organ of speech, the nose, the eyes, the ears, the mind and the vital force to chant hymns for them. All sang successively. The demons immediately realised that the gods would, without fail, gain supremacy over them through these chanters, so they secretly and successfully contaminated them with the blatant evil of strong attachment to sense objects and the life of pleasure. They immediately succeeded with the organ of speech, the nose, the eyes, the ears and the mind. But to the vital force they lost badly. The vital force broke them into pieces and threw them in all directions. The vital force won the victory for the gods. Their existence was inundated with Divinity's eternal Light. They became their true selves. The chicanery of the jealous demons was exposed, and their pride was smashed (*Chāndogyopaniṣad* I.2.1-9).

This vital force is called *ayāsya āṅgirasa.** It means the essence of the limbs. The vital force was victorious. It was also kind, sympathetic and generous.

The vital force carried the organ of speech beyond the domain of death. Having transcended the region of death, the organ of speech became fire, and this fire shines far beyond death.

The vital force carried the nose beyond death. The nose then became the air. Having transcended the boundaries of death, the air blows beyond death.

The vital force carried the eyes beyond death. The eyes became the sun. Having transcended the region of death, the sun perpetually shines.

The vital force carried the ears beyond death. They then became the directions. These directions,

---

*See *Bṛhadāraṇyakopaniṣad* I.3.8 and *Chāndogyopaniṣad* I.2.10–12; also *Ṛgveda* X.67.1.

having transcended death, remain far beyond its domain.

The vital force carried the mind beyond death. The mind then became the moon. The moon, having transcended death, shines beyond its domain. (*Bṛhadāraṇyakopaniṣad* I.3.12-16)

The Bṛhadāraṇyaka, or 'great forest', Upanishad offers to humanity an unparalleled prayer :

Asato mā sad gamaya
Tamaso mā jyotir gamaya
Mṛtyor māmṛtaṃ gamaya
(*Bṛhadāraṇyakopaniṣad* I.3.28)

Lead me from the unreal to the Real.
Lead me from darkness to Light.
Lead me from death to Immortality.

The unreal is the frown of death; the Real is the song of Immortality. Darkness is the colossal pride of death; Light is the life of the illumining and perfecting power of Immortality. Death is the message of nothingness. Immortality is the message of humanity's liberated oneness with Divinity's transcendental Height.

University of California
Berkeley, California

The Beauty and Duty of India's Soul

This beauty is not tempting.
This beauty is illumining.
This duty is not self-imposed.
This duty is God-ordained.

The Upanishads offer us self-knowledge, world-knowledge and God-knowledge. Self-knowledge is self-discovery. After self-discovery we have to feel that world-knowledge is within us, and we have to grow into world-knowledge. When we know the Possessor of world-knowledge, we have God-knowledge. We have to enter into God-knowledge, which is the Possessor of the universe.

Neti neti—'Not this, not this' or 'Not this, not that'—is the message of the Upanishads.* All of us here are seekers of the infinite Truth. A real seeker is not and cannot be satisfied with his individual life, individual achievements, worldly possessions. No. He can be satisfied only when he has achieved the

*E.g. in *Bṛhadāraṇyakopaniṣad* II.3.6.

Absolute. What is the Absolute? Brahman is the Absolute.

The seers of the hoary past offered this sublime knowledge: "Brahman cannot be limited by anything, Brahman cannot be housed by anything, Brahman cannot be defined by anything." This is the negative way of seeing Brahman. There is a positive way, and this positive way is this: "Brahman is eternal, Brahman is infinite, Brahman is immortal. Brahman is beyond and beyond." We, the seekers of the infinite Truth, will follow the positive way. If we follow the positive way in our life of aspiration, we can run the fastest and reach the ultimate Goal sooner.

We have to see Brahman in the finite as we wish to see Brahman in the Infinite. During our meditation if we can have the vision of Brahman as the infinite Self, then it becomes easier for us to enter into the world of relativity where we see everything as finite.

We see the world within us; we see the world without us. In the world within there is a being, and in the world without there is also a being. These two beings are called 'non-being' and 'being.' From non-being, being came into existence. This very idea baffles our minds. How can non-being create being? Non-being is nothing. From nothing, how can something come into existence? But we have to know that it is the mind which tells us that from non-being being cannot come into existence. We have to know that this 'nothing' is actually something beyond the conception of the mind. 'Nothing' is the life of the everlasting Beyond. 'Nothing' is something that always remains beyond our mental conception. It transcends our limited consciousness. When we think of the world or of being coming out of non-being, we have to feel that this Truth can be known and realised only on the strength of our inner aspiration, where the mind does not operate at all. It is intuition which grants us this boon of knowing that 'nothing' is the song of the ever-transcending Beyond, and 'nothing' is the experience of the ever-fulfilling, ever-transcending and ever-manifesting existence.

The Upanishads and the essence of *prāṇa* are inseparable. *Prāṇa* is a Sanskrit word. It may be translated into English in various ways. It may be called 'breath' or 'energy' or even 'ether'. *Prāṇa* is life-energy. This life-energy is not material, it is not physical, but it is something that maintains and sustains the physical body. The source of *prāṇa* is the Supreme. In the field of manifestation *prāṇa* is indispensable. *Prāṇa* is the soul of the universe.

In India the term '*prāṇa*' has a special significance of its own. *Prāṇa* is not just breath. Daily we breathe in and out thousands of times without paying any attention. But when we use the term '*prāṇa*', we think of the life-energy that is flowing within and without in our breath.

Prāṇa is divided into five parts: *prāṇa*, *apāna*, *samāna*, *vyāna* and *udāna*. The life-energy, life-force that is inside the physical eyes, nose and ears, we call *prāṇa*. The life-energy in our organs of excretion and generation is *apāna*. *Samāna* is the life-energy that governs our digestion and assimilation. In the lotus of the heart, where the Self is located, we see one hundred and one subtle spiritual nerves, and in each nerve one hundred nerve branches, and from each nerve branch seventy-two thousand nerve branches. There the *prāṇa* that moves is called *vyāna*. Through the centre of the spine, life-energy flows. When it goes upward it reaches the Highest, and when it goes downward it reaches the lowest. When a seeker of the infinite Truth leaves the body, this *prāṇa* rises towards the Highest, and when a sinful person leaves the body, this *prāṇa* goes downward. This *prāṇa* which flows through the centre of the spine is called *udāna*.

When we are in a position to enter into the cosmos with the help of our life-force, we feel that the Beyond is not in our imagination. It is not a chimerical mist; it is a reality that is growing within us and for us. God was One. He wanted to be many. Why? He felt the necessity of enjoying Himself divinely and supremely in infinite forms. *Ekam aikṣata bahu syām*,* 'One desiring to be many', was His

---

*Cf. *Chāndogyopaniṣad* VI.2.3, where it is said, *tad aikṣata bahu syām prajāyeya*, "It [the One Being] saw and wished: may I become many, may I bring forth."

inner feeling. When the Supreme projected His Life-Energy, He saw two creatures immediately. One was male, the other female. *Prāṇa*, the life-force, is the male, and the female is *rayi*. *Prāṇa* is the sun. *Rayi* is the moon. From *prāṇa* and *rayi* we all came into existence. Again, *prāṇa* is spirit and *rayi* is matter. Spirit and matter must go together. Spirit needs matter for its self-manifestation, and matter needs spirit for its self-realisation.

Very often the Vedic and Upanishadic seers used two words: *nāma* and *rūpa*. *Nāma* is name; *rūpa* is form. In our outer world we deal with name and form. In the inner world we deal with the nameless and the formless. The name and the nameless are not rivals. The form and the formless are not rivals. The name embodies the capacity of the outer body. The nameless reveals the Immortality of the soul. In form, the Cosmic Consciousness manifests itself by circumscribing itself. In the formless, the Cosmic Consciousness transcends itself by expanding and enlarging itself.

In the spiritual life, the term 'sacrifice' is often used. The Vedic seers spoke elaborately on sacrifice. According to them, the horse sacrifice, the *aśvamedha* sacrifice, was most important. The Bṛhadāraṇyaka Upanishad starts with the sacrificial horse:

> *Uṣā vā aśvasya medhyasya śiraḥ …*
> (*Bṛhadāraṇyakopaniṣad* I.1.1)

> The head of the sacrificial horse is verily the dawn; the eye of the sacrificial horse is the sun; the vital force, the air; the open mouth, the fire named *vaiśvānara*; the trunk, the year; the back, Heaven; the belly, the sky; the hoof, the earth; the flanks, the four directions; the ribs, the intermediate directions; the limbs, the seasons; the joints, the months and fortnights; the feet, the days and nights; the bones, the stars; the flesh, the clouds; the half-digested food (in the stomach), the sands; the arteries and veins, the rivers; the liver and spleen, the mountains; the hairs, the herbs and trees; the forepart, the rising sun; the hind part, the setting sun. Its yawn is lightning, its shaking body is thunder, its making water is rain, its neighing is indeed speech.
>
> (*Bṛhadāraṇyakopaniṣad* I.1.1)

Why did the Upanishadic seers, the Vedic seers, speak of the horse and not any other animal as the symbol of sacrifice? They realised the speed of the horse, the dynamism of the horse, the faithful and devoted qualities of the horse. Speed is necessary, dynamism is necessary, faithfulness and devotedness are necessary to realise and reveal the Absolute. That is why they chose the horse for religious rites and for help in their inner awakening.

Just by sacrificing a horse we cannot gain any divine merit. Far from it. We must meditate on the qualities of the horse and invoke these divine qualities to enter into us from Above. The Vedic and Upanishadic seers did this. They succeeded in getting the divine qualities from the horse, and the result was that they entered into *Brahmaloka*, the highest Heaven.

But even in the highest Heaven, the Delight we get is not everlasting. For everlasting Delight, we have to enter into Brahman on the strength of our inner cry. When we have the inner cry, we can eventually enter into Brahman and there get everlasting Delight.

To come back to the horse, one does not have to make a horse sacrifice in this age. But one has to see the qualities of the horse and inwardly meditate on the divinely fulfilling qualities of the horse. It is from one's own concentration and meditation that one will get the qualities which the horse offers or represents. Very often people misunderstand the idea of sacrifice, especially Westerners. They cannot understand how they can gain any divine merit just by killing a horse. They think it is absurd. But sacrifice is not merely killing. Sacrifice is in becoming one with the consciousness of the horse. When we do this, only then can we get the divine wealth from Above. We need not, we must not kill the horse at all.

To be sure, there can be no sacrifice without aspiration. At every moment aspiration is necessary. But this aspiration has to be genuine and has to come from the very depths of the heart. It cannot give us realisation if it is not genuine. Aspiration does not know how to pull or push. Restlessness and aspiration can never go together. Very often beginners think that if they aspire they have to be very dynamic. This is true. But we do not see dynamism in their aspiration. What we see is restlessness. They want to realise God overnight. If we take this restlessness as determination or dynamism, then we are totally mistaken.

May I repeat an oft-quoted story? A seeker went to a spiritual Master. He was properly initiated, and in a few days' time this seeker said to the Master, "Master, now that you have initiated me, please give me God-realisation." The Master said, "You have to practise meditation for a long time." After a few days the disciple again said, "Master, Master, give me realisation, please give me realisation." He bothered the Master for a long time. One day the Master asked him to follow him. The Master went to the Ganges for a dip and invited the disciple also to enter the water. When the disciple was neck-deep in water, the Master pushed his head underwater and held it there. When the Master finally let the struggling disciple come up, he asked him, "What did you feel while you were underwater?" The disciple replied, "O Master, I felt that I would die if I did not get a breath of air." The Master said, "You will realise God on the day you feel that you will die if He does not come and give you life. If you sincerely feel that you will die without God, if you can cry for Him in that way, then you are bound to realise Him."

The Master offered this truth to the disciple. Unfortunately we very often see that when a Master offers the Truth, the disciples misunderstand. They understand it according to their limited light, or they feel that the message the Master has given is totally wrong. If the Truth that is offered by the Master is not properly understood and used, then in the field of manifestation the seeker will never be fulfilled. The highest Truth will always remain a far cry for him.

In the Upanishads, Indra and Virocana went to Prajāpati for the highest Knowledge (*Chāndogyopaniṣad* VIII.7-12). Indra represented the gods, and Virocana represented the demons. When Prajāpati offered them the knowledge of Brahman, Indra went back again and again to verify the knowledge he had received, and he finally did realise the highest Knowledge. But Virocana understood the Truth in his own way, and did not feel the necessity of going back again and again to realise the highest Truth.

There are quite a few spiritual Masters on earth who are offering their light to seekers, but the seekers unfortunately do not understand the message of Truth which they offer. How can they understand the message, the meaning, the significance of the Truth which the Master offers? They can do it only on the strength of their devotion—devotion to the cause, and devotion to the Master. If they have a devoted feeling toward their Master and toward the cause of self-realisation, then the Truth can be realised in the way the Truth has to be realised, and the message that the Master offers to chase away ignorance will be not only properly understood, but also established in the earth atmosphere. When Truth is permanently established here on earth, man will receive the garland of eternal Victory.

New York University
New York, New York

Glimpses from the Vedas and the Upanishads

Nālpe sukham asti bhūmaiva sukham
(*Chāndogyopaniṣad* VII.23.1)

In the finite there is no happiness.
The Infinite alone is happiness.

Anything that is finite cannot embody happiness, not to speak of lasting delight. The finite embodies pleasure, which is not true happiness. The Infinite embodies true divine happiness in infinite measure, and at the same time, it reveals and offers to the world at large its own truth, its own wealth.

The Infinite expresses itself in infinite forms and infinite shapes here in the world of multiplicity; and again this Infinite enjoys itself in a divine and supreme manner in the highest transcendental plane of its own consciousness. The Infinite here in the world of multiplicity expresses itself in three major forms. Creation is the first aspect of the Infinite. The second aspect is preservation. The third aspect is dissolution or destruction.

These terms—'creation', 'preservation' and 'destruction'—are philosophical and religious terms. From the spiritual point of view, creation existed, does exist and is being preserved. When we use the term 'destruction', we have to be very careful. In the Supreme's inner Vision, destruction is nothing but transformation. When we lose our desires, we feel that they have been destroyed. But they have not been destroyed—they have only been transformed into a larger vision, which is aspiration. We started our journey with desire, but when we launched into the spiritual path, desire gave way to aspiration. The unlit consciousness which we see in the form of desire can be transformed and will be transformed by the aspiration within us. What we call destruction, with our limited knowledge and vision, from the spiritual point of view is the transformation of our unlit, impure, obscure nature.

Ekam evādvitīyam (*Chāndogyopaniṣad* VI.2.1)

Only the One, without a second.

From this One we came into existence, and at the end of our journey's close we have to return to the Absolute One. This is the soul's journey. If we take it as an outer journey, then we are mistaken. In our outer journey we have a starting point and a final destination. It may take a few years or many years for us to reach our destined goal, for the starting point is at one place and the destination is somewhere else. But the inner journey is not a journey as such, with the origin here and the goal elsewhere. In our inner journey we go deep within and discover our own Reality, our own forgotten Self.

How do we discover our forgotten Self? We do it through meditation. There are various types of meditation: simple meditation, which everybody knows; deep meditation, which the spiritual seeker knows; and higher or highest meditation, which is the meditation of the soul, in the soul, with the soul, for the entire being. When an ordinary seeker meditates, he meditates in the mind. If he is a little advanced in the spiritual life, he meditates in the heart. If he is far advanced in the spiritual life, he can meditate in the soul and with the help of the soul for the manifestation of Divinity in humanity.

Spiritual Masters meditate in the physical, in the vital, in the mind, in the heart and in the souls of their disciples. These Masters also meditate all at once on the Infinite, Eternal and Immortal. These are not vague terms to the real spiritual Masters. They are dynamic realities, for in their inner consciousness, real spiritual Masters swim in the sea of Infinity, Eternity and Immortality. They can easily concentrate, meditate and contemplate on these three divine realities which represent the Absolute.

The Upanishads have come into existence from four Vedas: the Rig Veda, the Sama Veda, the Yajur Veda and the Atharva Veda. Each Veda has something unique to offer to mankind. The first and most famous Veda is the Rig Veda. It starts with a cosmic god, Agni, the fire god. Fire means aspiration. Aspiration and the message of the Vedas are inseparable. This fire is the fire of inner awakening, the inner mounting flame. It creates no smoke and does not burn anything; it only illumines and elevates our consciousness. The fire god is the only cosmic god who is a Brahmin. Agni, fire, expresses itself in seven forms and has seven significant inner names: *Kālī*, the black; *Karālī*, the terrible; *Manojavā*, thought-swift; *Sulohitā*, blood-red; *Sudhūmravarṇā*, smoke-hued; *Sphuliṅginī*, scattering sparks; *Viśvarucī*, the all-beautiful (*Muṇḍakopaniṣad* 1.2.4).

Kali, the black, is not actually black. Kali is the divine force or fire within us which fights against undivine hostile forces. Mother Kali fights against demons in the battlefield of life. In the vital plane we see Her as a dark, tenebrous Goddess, but in the highest plane of consciousness She is golden. We see Her terrible form when She fights against hostile forces, but She is the Mother of compassion. We misunderstand Her dynamic qualities—we take them as aggressive qualities. Mother Kali has compassion in boundless measure, but at the same time, She will not tolerate any sloth, imperfection, ignorance or lethargy in the seeker. Finally, Mother Kali is beauty unparalleled. This beauty is not physical beauty. This beauty is inner beauty, which elevates human consciousness to the highest plane of Delight.

The Sama Veda offers us God's music, the soul's music. In addition, it offers India's religion, India's philosophy and India's politics. All these striking achievements of India have come from the Sama Veda. Music is of paramount importance in the Sama Veda. It is not at all like modern music; it is the real soul-stirring music. The greatest sage of the past, Yājñavalkya, said, "The abode of music is Heaven." It is the Sama Veda which holds this Heavenly music—the soul-stirring, life-energising music.

Most of you have read the Bhagavad Gita, the Song Celestial of Lord Krishna. There Lord Krishna says, "I am the Sama Veda." (*Bhagavad Gītā* 10.22) He does not say that he is the Rig Veda or the Yajur Veda or the Atharva Veda. No, he says that he is the Sama Veda. Why? Because in the Sama Veda Krishna found the soul's music, which is his very own. A great Indian philosopher-saint, Patañjali, begins his philosophy with the Sama Veda precisely because of its inner music. If music is taken away from God's creation, then it will be an empty creation. God the Creator is the Supreme Musician, and His creation is His only Delight. It is in His music that God feels Delight, and it is through music that He offers Himself to His aspiring and unaspiring children.

From the Sama Veda we get the most significant Upanishad, the Chāndogya Upanishad. This

Upanishad is equal to the Bṛhadāraṇyaka Upanishad. It is by far the largest in size, and according to many, it is not only the largest but also the best. Again, there are those who are of the opinion that the Īśā Upanishad, which is very tiny, is the best—not because of its size, but because of its depth. Some will say the Śvetāśvatara or Kaṭha or Kena Upanishad is the best. Each one has to express his sincere feeling about the essence of a particular Upanishad.

The Chāndogya Upanishad, which derives from the Sama Veda, says something most significant to the sincere seekers. One question which spiritual teachers are very often asked is, "Why do we need a teacher? Can we not realise God by ourselves?" In the Chāndogya Upanishad there is a specific way of convincing the doubters and the unaspiring human beings who argue for the sake of argument. The Chāndogya Upanishad (*Chāndogyopaniṣad* VI.14.1-2) says to think of yourself as a traveller. You have lost your way, and a robber attacks you. He takes away all your wealth and binds your eyes. Then he takes you to a faraway place and leaves you there. Originally you had vision, and you were able to move around, but now your fate is deplorable. You cannot see, you cannot walk, you are crying like a helpless child, but there is no rescue.

Now suppose someone comes and unties your eyes and goes away. You will then be able to see the paths all around you, but you will not know which one is the right one for you, and even if you did, you would not be able to walk on it because your legs and arms are still bound. This is the condition of the seeker who wants to realise God by himself. But suppose someone comes, unties you completely and shows you which path will take you home. This person has really done you a favour. If you have faith in him and confidence in yourself, then you will reach your destination swiftly and surely. If you have faith in him, but do not have confidence in your own capacity to reach the goal, then he will go along to help you. The same teacher who freed you from blindness and showed you the path will go with you, inside you, to inspire you. He will act as your own aspiration to lead you toward your destined Goal.

If you get this kind of help from a spiritual Master, then your life can be of significance, your life can bear fruit, and you can run the fastest toward the Goal. Otherwise, you will walk today on this path, tomorrow on that path, and the following day on some other path. You may have the capacity to walk, but you will come back again and again to your starting point, frustrated and disappointed. Along with capacity, if you know the right path and have a true Master to help you, who can prevent you from reaching your destined Goal? Once you reach your destined Goal, you reach God's Heights and start manifesting God's Light here on earth. You are fulfilled—fulfilled multiplicity in unity's embrace.

Fairleigh Dickinson University
Teaneck, New Jersey

The Crown of India's Soul

In the silent recesses of the Upanishadic heart, we see and feel a splendid combination of the soul's spirituality and life's practicality. In the world of imagination, in the world of aspiration, in the world of realisation, in the world of revelation and in the world of manifestation, the soul of the Upanishads has the divine effrontery to assume the sovereign leadership, because that is its natural role. Its understanding embraces all the foibles of weak humanity. Its universal love is the song of self-offering.

The Upanishads are at once the heart's aspiration-cry and the soul's experience-smile. They have the vision of unity in multiplicity. They are the manifestation of multiplicity in unity.

The message of the Upanishads is the life divine, the life of transformed humanity and the life of an illumined earth-consciousness. The Upanishads tell us that the renunciation of desire-life is the fulfilling enjoyment of world-existence. This renunciation is neither self-denial nor self-rejection. This renunciation demands the transcendence of ego, to breathe in freely the life-energy of the soul and yet to live a dynamic and active life in the world, where one can achieve Infinity's Height, Eternity's Delight and Immortality's Light.

Each major Upanishad is a pathfinder in the forest of experience that comprises human life. Each major Upanishad offers us the intuitive knowledge and the inner courage to find our way through the labyrinth of curves and dead ends, doubts and subterfuges. We come to realise that life is a glorious adventure of the aspiring heart, searching mind, struggling vital and unsleeping body. We explore the hidden places of illumining individuality and fulfilling personality. Gone is our mind's obscurity. Gone is our heart's poverty. Gone is our vital's impurity. Gone is our body's insincerity. The train of Light has arrived. The plane of Delight has come.

The Upanishads teach the seeker that Delight is the manifestation of divine Love, Consciousness is the manifestation of the soul-force and Existence is the manifestation of Being. In Delight, Brahman is Reality. In Love, Brahman is Divinity. In Consciousness, Brahman contemplates the Vision of perfect Perfection. In the soul-force, Brahman becomes the achievement of perfect Perfection. In Existence, Brahman is the eternal Lover. In Being, Brahman is the eternal Beloved.

For God-realisation we need a Guru. The Kaṭha Upanishad (*Kaṭhopaniṣad* 1.2.8) says, "A seeker cannot find his way to God unless he is told of God by another." The Muṇḍaka Upanishad (*Muṇḍakopaniṣad* 1.2.12) says, "A seeker must approach a Self-knower for his inner illumination." The Praśna Upanishad (*Praśnopaniṣad* 6.8) says, "O Father, you have carried us over to the Golden Shore." The Kaṭha Upanishad (*Kaṭhopaniṣad* 1.3.14) says, "Arise, awake! Listen to and follow the great ones." The Muṇḍaka Upanishad (*Muṇḍakopaniṣad* 1.2.12) says, "A Guru is he whose outer knowledge is the Veda and whose inner knowledge is the contemplation of Brahman."

A seeker who studies the Upanishads and leads a life of self-enquiry and self-discipline is not and cannot be a mere player on the stage of life, but is rather a spiritual art director and a real divine producer. Further, he has two broad shoulders and does not mind the burdens of the world. He feels that it is his obligation to assuage the bleeding heart of humanity. His life is the independence of thought and spirit. His heart's dedicated service receives rich rewards from Above. He has mastered his own philosophy of life, which is to please Divinity in humanity.

> *Taccakṣur devahitaṃ śukram uccarat paśyema śaradaḥ satam* (*Ṛgveda* VII.66.16)

> May we, for a hundred autumns, see that lustrous Eye, God-ordained, arise before us.

To live a hundred years is not just to drag out our existence here on earth. One has to fight against ignorance. Desultory efforts cannot carry us to God.

It takes time to realise God. It takes more time to reveal God. It takes even more time to manifest God. That is why the seers of the Vedas prayed for sound health and long life, a life beyond a hundred autumns. They also warned us that anything that is deleterious to our health has to be avoided.

Uru ṇas tanve tan
Uru kṣayāya nas kṛdhi
Uru ṇo yaṃdhi jīvase (*Ṛgveda* VIII.68.12)

For our body give us freedom.
For our dwelling give us freedom.
For our life give us freedom.

Vivekananda, the great Vedāntin of indomitable courage, voiced forth, "Freedom—physical freedom, mental freedom and spiritual freedom—is the watchword of the Upanishads."

In order to achieve freedom, we need energy, power and spirit. And for that, here is the mightiest prayer:

Tejo 'si tejo mayi dhehi
Vīryam asi vīryam mayi dhehi
Balam asi balaṃ mayi dhehi
Ojo 'si ojo mayi dhehi
Manyur asi manyur mayi dhehi
Saho 'si saho mayi dhehi
(*Yajurveda, Vājasaneyisaṃhitā* 19.9)

Thy fiery spirit I invoke.
Thy manly vigour I invoke.
Thy power and energy I invoke.
Thy battle fury I invoke.
Thy conquering mind I invoke.

The Upanishads always hold the intrepid view of life. Progress, constant progress, is the characteristic of the Vedic and Upanishadic age.

Prehi abhīhi dhṛṣṇuhi (*Ṛgveda* I.80.3)

Go forward, fear not, fight!

Fight against what? Bondage, ignorance and death. Life is ours. Victory must needs be ours too. Anything that stands in the seeker's way has to be thrown aside without hesitation. His is the life that knows no compromise.

The main longing of the Upanishads is for the ultimate Truth. This Truth can be achieved by a genuine seeker who has many divine qualities and whose love of God preponderates over every other love. The seeker needs three things: *vrata*, self-dedication; *kṛpā*, grace; and *śraddhā*, faith. These three qualities embodied, *satya*, Truth, is unmistakably attained.

Who wants to remain alone? No one, not even the highest, the first-born, Virāṭ. There came a time when He felt the need of projecting the cosmic gods. He projected the Fire God, Agni, the only

Brahmin god, from His mouth. Indra, Varuṇa, Yama, Īśāna and others were projected from His arms. These are the Kshatriya gods. Then He projected the Vasus, the Rudras, the Maruts and others from His thighs. These are the Vaishya gods. He projected Pūṣan from His feet. Pūṣan is the Shudra god.*

A Brahmin embodies knowledge. A Kshatriya embodies strength. A Vaishya embodies prosperity. A Shudra embodies the secret of self-dedication. These four brothers are the limbs of the Cosmic Being. Although they are outwardly distinguishable by their quality and capacity, in spirit they are inseparably one.

Brahman, or the Supreme Self, is the greatest discovery of the Upanishads. No human soul knows or will ever know when ignorance entered into us, for earth-bound time itself is the creation of ignorance. Still, a man swimming in the sea of ignorance need not drown. The seers of the hoary past, the knowers of the Brahman, in unmistakable terms tell us that all human beings can and must come out of the shackles of ignorance. The knowers of the transcendental Truth also tell us that the individual soul is in reality identical with the Supreme Self. The only problem is that the individual does not remem-

---

**Bṛhadāraṇyakopaniṣad* I.4.11–I.14.15; see also the famous *Puruṣa* hymn in *Ṛgveda* X.90.

ber his true transcendental nature. Finally they tell us that "to know the Self is to become the Self." On the strength of his direct realisation, a knower of Brahman declares, *Aham Brahmāsmi*, "I am Brahman." (*Bṛhadāraṇyakopaniṣad* I.4.10)

The mind-power, the heart-power and the soul-power of the Upanishadic consciousness are boundless. In the realm of philosophy, Shankara embodies the mind-power; in the realm of dynamic spirituality, Ramana Maharshi, the great sage of Arunachala, embodies the mind-power. The Christ, the Buddha and Sri Chaitanya of Nadia, Bengal, embody the heart-power. Sri Krishna and Sri Ramakrishna embody the soul-power. In Sri Aurobindo the vision of the mind-power reached its zenith, and the realisation of the soul-power found its fulfilling manifestation on earth. These spiritual giants and others are steering the life-boat of humanity towards the transcendental Abode of the Supreme.

Harvard University
Cambridge, Massachusetts

The Brahman of the Upanishads

The heart of the Upanishads is most meaningful and most fruitful because it embodies the life of Brahman. Brahman is Reality in existence; Brahman is Reality's existence. The eternal Truth of Brahman is in the finite, beyond the finite, in the Infinite and beyond the ever-transcending Infinite.

In the domain of realisation, Brahman is the Sovereign Absolute. In the domain of revelation, Brahman is the omnipresent Reality. In the field of manifestation, Brahman is the immortalising Perfection.

Brahman the Creator is Consciousness-Light; Brahman the Fulfiller is Consciousness-Delight. Brahman is the inner Soul of all and the only Goal in all.

When we look within, Brahman is Consciousness-Force. When we look without, Brahman is Self-manifestation. When we think of Brahman with the earth-bound mind, the limited mind, the unaspiring mind, our life becomes sheer frustration. When we meditate on Brahman in the silent recesses of the heart, our life becomes pure illumination.

To a non-seeker, Brahman is unknowable. To a beginner-seeker, Brahman is unknown. To a Master-seeker, Brahman is knowable, Brahman is known. Further, the Master himself grows into the Consciousness of Brahman.

> *Sarvaṃ khalvidaṃ brahma*
> (*Chāndogyopaniṣad* III.14.1)
>
> Indeed, all is Brahman.

The Eternal is existence within. The Eternal is existence without.

There is no abiding happiness in the finite. It is only in the Infinite that we can hear the message of eternal Delight. *Ānandaṃ Brahma* and *Anantaṃ Brahma* are the two major aspects of Brahman. *Ānandaṃ Brahma* is the life of the all-illumining and all-fulfilling Delight. *Anantaṃ Brahma* is the life of Infinity.

Here on earth the life of Infinity constantly grows for the fulfilment of the Absolute Brahman. That is why the Upanishadic seers sing from the depths of their hearts about the transcendental Delight of Brahman:

> *Ānandāddhyeva khalvimāni bhūtāni jāyante*
> *Ānandena jātāni jīvanti*
> *Ānandaṃ prayantyabhisaṃviśanti*
> (*Taittirīyopaniṣad* III.6)

From the transcendental Delight
we came into existence.
In Delight we grow
and play our respective roles.
At the end of our journey's close,
we enter into the supreme Delight.

Again, when the seers saw Infinity in Brahman, they sang:

Pūrṇam adaḥ pūrṇam idaṃ pūrṇāt pūrṇam udacyate
Pūrṇasya pūrṇam ādāya pūrṇam evāvaśiṣyate
(Invocation from the *Īśopaniṣad* and *Bṛhadāraṇyakopaniṣad*)

Infinity is that. Infinity is this.
From Infinity, Infinity has come into existence.
From Infinity, when Infinity is taken away, Infinity remains.

Brahman is active. Brahman is inactive. The active Brahman inwardly does and outwardly becomes. Also, the active Brahman outwardly does and inwardly becomes. But the inactive Brahman is the total freedom of inaction and complete freedom in inaction.

Brahman is at once the eternal Unborn and the eternal birth and growth of existence. Brahman is ignorance-night. Brahman is knowledge-light. Brahman the ignorance-night needs total transformation. Brahman the knowledge-light needs complete manifestation.

The whole universe came into existence from Brahman the Seed. When Brahman wanted to project Himself, He first projected Himself through four significant worlds: *Ambhas*, the highest world; *Marīci*, the sky; *Mara*, the mortal world, the earth; and *Apa*, the world beneath earth.* Then Brahman sent forth the guardians of these worlds. Next, He sent forth food for them. Then Brahman came to realise that He Himself had to take part in His Cosmic Game, so He entered into the Cosmic *Līlā* (game) through His own yogic power. First He entered into the human body through the skull. The door by which Brahman entered is called the door of Delight. This door is the highest centre of consciousness. It is known as *sahasrāra*, the thousand-petaled lotus. It is situated in the centre of the brain. The realisation of the yogi enters there and becomes one with the Consciousness of Brahman.

Brahman has many names, but His secret name is 'Aum'.

> *Praṇavo dhanuḥ śāro hyātmā brahma tallakṣyam*
> (*Muṇḍakopaniṣad* 2.2.4)

---

*This series of worlds is a very old Vedic list and was later replaced by the concept of seven higher worlds and seven lower worlds.

Aum is the bow and *ātman,* the self, is the arrow; Brahman is the target.

Through repeated practice the arrow is fixed into the target, the Brahmic Consciousness. Through regular concentration, meditation and contemplation, the seeker enters into the Absolute Consciousness of Brahman.

Creation is the supreme sacrifice of Brahman. Creation is by no means a mechanical construction. Creation is a spiritual act, supremely revealing, manifesting and fulfilling the divine splendour of Brahman. The divine Architect is beyond creation, and at the same time manifests Himself in and through creation.

Brahman created out of His Being priests, warriors, tradesmen and servants. Then He created the Law. Nothing can be higher than this Law. This Law is Truth. When a man speaks the Truth, he declares the Law. When he declares the Law, he speaks the Truth. The Truth and the Law are one, inseparable.

Indian mythology has divided Time—not earth-bound time but eternal Time—into four divisions: *satyayuga*, *tretayuga*, *dvāparayuga* and *kaliyuga*. According to many we are now in the *kaliyuga*. Brahman in the *kaliyuga* is fast asleep. He is in inconscience-ignorance-mire. In the *dvāparayuga* He awakes and He looks around. In the *tretayuga* He stands up, about to move forward. In the *satyayuga*, the golden age, He moves fast, faster, fastest towards His Goal.* The message of the Vedas, the eternal message of Aryan culture and civilisation,** the realisation of the Indian sages and seers, is movement, inner progress, life's march towards the destined Goal.

> *Caraiveti caraiveti*
> *(Aitareyabrāhmaṇa* 7.15*)*
>
> Move on, move on!

Yale University
New Haven, Connecticut

**Aitareyabrāhmaṇa* 7.15.5

**The old Vedic Indians called themselves *'Āryāḥ'*, meaning 'the noble ones'. They called their land on the Ganges *'Āryāvarta'* (land of the Aryas). Therefore the north Indian culture and north Indian languages are often called Aryan culture or Aryan languages.

The Gāyatrī Mantra

Aum bhūr bhuvaḥ svaḥ
Tat savitur vareṇyam
Bhargo devasya dhīmahi
Dhiyo yo naḥ pracodayāt (*Ṛgveda* III.62.10)*

We meditate on the transcendental Glory of the Deity Supreme, who is inside the heart of the earth, inside the life of the sky and inside the soul of the Heaven. May He stimulate and illumine our minds.

The Gāyatrī Mantra is the most hallowed mantra of the Vedas. It is the mother of all mantras. Mantra means incantation. A mantra can be a one-syllable word or a few words, a sentence or a few sentences. The Gāyatrī Mantra can offer to the sincere seeker

---

*Here again Sri Chinmoy uses '*Aum*' instead of the more common '*Om*'. See the explanation on page 23. The first line here (*Aum bhūr bhuvaḥ svaḥ*) consists of the mantra *Aum* and the so-called 'great *Vyāhṛti*', the enumeration of the first three of the seven worlds (see note on page 4), which in this form often precedes the mantras for the sacrifice.

the Light of the Infinite, the Delight of the Eternal and the Life of the Immortal.

The Gāyatrī Mantra has four feet. The first foot consists of the earth, sky and Heaven. The second foot consists of the Rig Veda, the Yajur Veda and the Sama Veda. The third foot consists of *prāṇa, apāna* and *vyāna*. The fourth foot consists of the sun, the Solar Being.

A seeker of the infinite Truth must meditate on the Gāyatrī Mantra. The result that he will get is incalculable.

Bhūmi, earth; *antarikṣa*, sky; and *dyauḥ*, Heaven, make up the first foot of the Gāyatrī Mantra. Whoever realises the significance of the first foot wins everything that is in those three worlds.

Ṛcaḥ, *Yajūṁṣi* and *Sāmāni** make up the second foot of the Gāyatrī Mantra. Whoever realises the second foot of the Gāyatrī wins the knowledge-sea of the three Vedas.

Prāṇa, apāna and *vyāna*, the three forms of the vital force, make up the third foot of the Gāyatrī Mantra. The knower of this foot wins all the living creatures that exist in the universe.

Turīyam, the quaternary, the Solar Being Transcendental who alone shines, is the fourth foot. He who realises this fourth foot shines with infinite magnificence.

**Ṛcaḥ*, *Yajūṁṣi* and *Sāmāni* are the verses of the Rig, Yajur and Sama Veda respectively.

Subtle is the path to *mokṣa*, liberation. Hard is the path to liberation. But a genuine seeker can reach the Goal solely by meditating on the Gāyatrī Mantra. When one is freed from the fetters of ignorance, one grows into the supernal glory of the Transcendental Self. Liberation can be achieved, must be achieved, while the seeker's soul is in the body. To fail to realise God on earth is to swim in the sea of ignorance with two more swimmers: ignorant birth and shameless death. Liberation attained, the bonds of grief destroyed. Before liberation, like the Buddha we have to proclaim, "This fleeting world is the abode of sorrow."*

The teeming desire-night that has occupied the heart of the seeker must needs be driven out by the glowing aspiration-light. This done, the seeker attains Brahman. Immortal he becomes. The Light eternal is his new name. Today the seeker feels that the Gāyatrī Mantra is his mind's inspiration. Tomorrow he will feel that the Gāyatrī Mantra is his soul's realisation.

With inspiration a seeker sees the Truth. With aspiration a seeker realises the Truth. With realisation a seeker becomes the Truth.

Inspiration is might.
Aspiration is light.
Realisation is life.

---

*This is the first of the Four Noble Truths taught by the Buddha.

Inspiration runs.
Aspiration flies.
Realisation dives.

Inspiration is the Smile of God.
Aspiration is the Cry of God.
Realisation is the Love of God.

The Gāyatrī Mantra is eternal knowledge divine. When this knowledge dawns in the seeker's aspiring heart, he need no longer seek anything, either on earth or in Heaven. He reveals what he achieves. He manifests what he reveals.

In the Vedas there are two most significant words: *satya* and *ṛta*. *Satya* is Truth in its pure existence. *Ṛta* is Truth in its dynamic movement. There is another word, *bṛhat*, which means vastness in form. What we call creation is the manifestation of the Unmanifest, *asat*. According to our scriptures, the manifestation took place with the *anāhatadhvani*, the soundless sound, Aum.

The Gāyatrī Mantra is dedicated to Savitṛ, the Creator. The root of the word Savitṛ is *su*—'to create' or 'to loose forth'. This mantra is known also as the Sāvitrī Mantra, for Sāvitrī is the shakti* of Savitṛ. This mantra was envisioned by Viśvāmitra, the great

---

**Shakti* means 'power' or 'capacity'. The shakti of a god is his own aspect of creative and effective power, and in mythology it is represented as his consort.

rishi. Savitṛ is regarded as Brahma, Vishnu and Shiva. Brahma, the Creator, with Brahmānī as his shakti; Vishnu, the Preserver, with his shakti, Vaiṣṇavī; and Shiva or Rudra, the Destroyer, with his shakti, Rudrāṇī, regularly visit the Brahman. The eagle is the vehicle-bird of Vishnu. The swan is the vehicle-bird of Brahma. The bull is the vehicle-beast of Shiva.

The Gāyatrī Mantra is the divine magnetic needle. The magnetic needle points to the north; hence the ship does not lose its direction. The Gāyatrī Mantra always points to the transcendental Height of the Supreme, hence the seeker does not miss his Goal: Existence, Consciousness, Bliss.

Columbia University
New York, New York

The Journey's Start, the Journey's Close

Human aspiration is the journey's start. Divine manifestation is the journey's close. Birthless is the journey's birth, and endless is the journey's end.

We came; we shall return. We came from the Supreme Being. To the Supreme Being we shall return. We embody the earth-consciousness and the Heaven-consciousness. The earth-consciousness inspires us to meditate on the transcendental Truth and realise the transcendental Truth in the soul of Heaven. The Heaven-consciousness inspires us to meditate on love and manifest love in the heart of earth.

We know, we grow and we become. We know in Heaven. We grow here on earth. We become the transcendental Truth. What we know is Reality. What we grow into is Immortality. What we eventually become is Divinity's Perfection. Reality embodies Immortality and Divinity. Immortality and Divinity manifest Reality.

The Upanishads teach us the significant truth

that each individual seeker must have inner peace and outer freedom. It is only through inner peace that we can have true outer freedom. From the Upanishads we learn how to discover God, the inner man, and see man, the revealed God. The Upanishads tell us that dedicated human beings, surrendered human souls, are God's necessity, and each realised human being is given God's unreserved, infinite capacity.

Here is the secret of the Upanishads: love, serve and become. Love God's Life in man, serve God's Light in man, and become God's perfect Perfection here on earth.

In two words we can sum up the message of all the Upanishads: aspiration and manifestation. Aspiration is the way, and manifestation is the Goal. Aspiration is the song of the infinite, eternal Consciousness abiding within us. Manifestation is the dance of unity's multiplicity, within and without us. Aspiration is the height of our Delight, and manifestation is the light of all-nourishing and all-fulfilling Delight.

Each soul needs involution and evolution. When the soul descends, it is the soul's involution. When the soul ascends, it is the soul's evolution. The soul enters into the lowest abyss of inconscience. The soul evolves again into *Saccidānanda*—Existence, Consciousness, Bliss—the triple consciousness.

The soul enters into inconscience. For millions of years it remains there, fast asleep. All of a sudden, one day a spark of consciousness from the ever-transcending Beyond opens its eye, and then the hour strikes for self-enquiry. "Who am I?" it asks. The answer is *Tat twam asi* (*Chāndogyopaniṣad* VI.8.7ff), "That thou art." The soul is thrilled. Then again it falls asleep. Again it enters into self-oblivion. More questions arise after some time:

> Whose am I? I am of That.
> Where have I come from? From That.
> To Whom am I returning? To That.
> For Whom am I here on earth? For That.

Then the soul is satisfied. The soul is now fully prepared for its journey upward—high, higher, highest. At this moment the soul sees the Self, an exact prototype of the Supreme Being here on earth, and the evolution of the soul starts properly. From the mineral life, the soul enters into the plant life, from the plant to the animal life, from the animal to the human life, and from the human into the divine life. While in the human life, the soul brings down peace, light and bliss from Above. First it offers these divine qualities to the heart, then to the mind, then to the vital, then to the gross physical. When illumination takes place, we see it in the heart, in the physical mind, in the vital and in the gross physical body.

The Upanishads are also called Vedānta. Vedānta means the end of the Vedas, the cream of the Vedas, the essence of the Vedas. It is said that Vedānta is the end of all difference—the point where there can be no difference between the lowest and the highest, between the finite and the Infinite.

Our journey starts with aspiration. What is aspiration? It is the inner cry, the inner hunger for the infinite Vast. Aspiration has a most sincere friend—concentration. How do we concentrate? Where do we concentrate? We concentrate on an object, on a being, on a form or on the formless. When we concentrate with the help of the mind, we feel that eventually we shall see the vastness of the Truth. When we concentrate with the help of the heart, we feel that one day we shall feel our intimacy with the universal Consciousness and God the eternal Beloved. When we concentrate with the help of our soul's light, we feel that man is God in His preparation, and God is man in his culmination.

The unaspiring mind is our real problem. The human mind is necessary to some extent. Without it we would remain in the animal domain. But we have to know that the human mind is very limited. The human mind is insufficient. In the human mind there cannot be any abiding light, life or delight. The human mind tells us that the finite is the finite, the Infinite is the Infinite, and there is a yawning gulf between the two. They are like the North Pole and the South Pole. Whatever is infinite can never be finite and vice-versa. Infinity, the human mind feels, is unattainable. When something is finite, it is simply impossible for the human mind to feel that that, too, is God. Also, this mind quite often feels that because of His greatness, God is aloof and indifferent.

When we meditate in the heart we come to realise that God is infinite and God is omnipotent. If He is infinite, on the strength of His omnipotence He can also be finite. He exists in our multifarious activities; He is everywhere. He includes everything; He excludes nothing. This is what our meditation can offer us. Our heart's meditation also tells us that God is dearer than the dearest and that He is our only Beloved.

Inspiration, aspiration and realisation—these are the three rungs of the spiritual ladder. When we want to climb from the finite to the Infinite with God's boundless Bounty, the first rung is inspiration, the second rung is aspiration and the third rung is realisation, our destined Goal.

To achieve the Highest, we become inspiration, aspiration and realisation; and to manifest the Highest here on earth, we become compassion, concern and love. This is how we start our journey; this is how we end our journey. Again, when we become inseparably one with the Inner Pilot, there is no beginning, there is no end. His Cosmic *Līlā*, divine Game, is birthless and endless.

In human realisation, God within us is aspiration and realisation bound by earth-consciousness, bound by earthly time. But in divine realisation, God is the Beyond, the ever-transcending Beyond. He plays the Game of the ever-transcending Beyond. He Himself is the aspiration of the ever-transcending Beyond, and He Himself is the manifestation of the ever-transcending Beyond. When we consciously know Him, realise Him, become inseparably one with Him, we too play His divine Game, the Game of Infinity, Eternity and Immortality.

Cornell University
Ithaca, New York

Life and Death, Ātman and Paramātman

The Upanishads come from the Vedas. They contain the records of eternal Truths. These Truths were discovered by various seers at different times and handed down to humanity.

Life is a problem. Even so is death. The aspiring Aryans of the hoary past wanted to solve these two problems. Soon they came to realise that their senses could be of almost no help to them in solving these two major problems. They also came to realise that it is the knowledge of the ultimate Reality alone that can solve, once and for all, the problems of life and death.

All of a sudden two divine soldiers came in. Nobody knows where they came from. These two soldiers were inspiration and aspiration. The first soldier, inspiration, commanded them: "Give up the study of the body." They immediately did so. The second soldier, aspiration, commanded them: "Take up the study of the soul." They immediately did so. Lo, the King and the Queen from the Golden Shore of the Beyond garlanded them, the seekers, the seers and the knowers of Light and Truth.

What do the Upanishads actually say? If you ask a Western seeker, he will immediately say, "Very simple. Sit at the feet of the Master and learn." If you ask an Eastern seeker the same question, he will quietly say, "Very difficult. Transform human darkness into divine Light." Both the Western and the Eastern seeker are perfectly right. No Master, no discovery of the transcendental Reality. No transformation of darkness, no manifestation of Divinity on earth.

Who needs the Truth? A seeker. When does he achieve the Truth? He achieves the Truth when he becomes the surrendered and divine lover.

His first achievement is God the Creator.
His second achievement is God the Preserver.
His third achievement is God the Transformer.
His fourth achievement is: Thou art That.
His fifth achievement is: I am That.
His sixth achievement is: He and I are one.
His seventh achievement is: He am I.

In the Creator he sees.
In the Preserver he feels.
In the Transformer he becomes.

The heart of the Upanishads is the *Puruṣa.* The life of the *Puruṣa* is the message of the Upanishads. Who is the *Puruṣa*? The *Puruṣa* is the real dweller in the body of the universe. The *Puruṣa* is three-fold: the outer *ātman*, the inner *Ātman* and the *Paramātman*.

The outer *ātman* is the gross physical body. The outer *ātman* is that which grows in the body, with the body and for the body. The outer *ātman* is the identification of one's body with the gross aspect of life. Here we live, we are hurt, we hurt others, we enjoy pleasure from others, we offer pleasure to others. This *ātman* exists, changes, develops and finally decays.

The inner *Ātman* is the discriminating Self. The inner *Ātman* identifies itself with the aspiring earth-consciousness. It identifies itself with air, ether, fire, water and earth. The inner *Ātman* is the thinker, the doer and the direct messenger of God. The inner *Ātman* manifests its inner realisation through outer experience.

The *Paramātman* reveals itself through the process of Yoga. Neither is it born, nor does it die. It is beyond all qualities. It is all-pervading, unimaginable and indescribable. It is Eternity's Reality, and Reality's Divinity.

Each Upanishad is a mighty drop from the fountain of eternal Life. This drop can easily cure the teeming ills of human life. The infinite power of this drop can free us from the endless rotation of human birth and death.

The mind, assisted by the body, creates bondage. The heart, assisted by the soul, offers liberation. The unaspiring mind thinks useless thoughts and down it sinks. It thinks too much and sinks too fast. The blind body is constantly digging its own grave. The heart wants to love and be loved. God gives the heart the life of oneness. The soul wants to reveal God. God fulfils the soul, and by doing so, He brings down the message of perfection in the divinity of manifested Reality.

Brown University
Providence, Rhode Island

Existence, Non-Existence and the Source

Sat and *asat* are two terms which one very often comes across in Indian philosophy. *Sat* means 'existence', and *asat* means 'non-existence'. Existence is something that becomes, grows and fulfils. Non-existence is something that negates its own reality and its own divinity. Existence is everywhere, but existence has its value or its meaning only when divinity is visible in it. If divinity does not loom large in existence, then that existence is useless. Divinity is the life-breath of existence. Divinity fulfils our aspiring consciousness and reveals our own Immortality here on earth only when we see divinity as something infinite and eternal.

Existence is cherished by the aspiring consciousness and by God's own highest Reality. Reality and existence have to go together. Reality without existence is an impossibility, and existence without reality is an absurdity. Divine Reality and divine Existence always go together.

Existence expresses itself only through Truth. This Truth conquers everything that is untruth.

India's motto, *Satyam eva jayate* (*Muṇḍakopaniṣad* 3.1.6), means 'Truth alone triumphs'. What is this Truth? This Truth is at once the Depth of God's Heart and the Height of God's Head.

Truth is our inner promise. Our inner promise, our soul's promise, is that in this incarnation we will realise God, not by hook or by crook, but under the able guidance of our spiritual Master, because we feel that this is what the Supreme within us wants. What for? So that we can serve Him in His own Way.

The highest way of feeling this Truth is to say, "If He does not want me to realise Him in this incarnation, but in some future incarnation, I am fully prepared to abide by His decision." But the seeker must have a dynamic feeling. If he just says, "Oh, let me play my role. Let me be nice, sincere, truthful, obedient, and when the time comes, He will do it all," then relaxation comes. Very often when we say, "Let me play my role, and God will take care of my realisation," God does take care of our realisation. But if we feel that if we can become fully realised as soon as possible, then we can be of real help to God, then we are bound to get our realisation faster.

Only if we have peace, light and bliss can we be of real service to humanity. The idea of God-realisation at God's choice Hour must come from the very depth of our heart, and not from our mental knowledge. Unfortunately, it usually does not come from the heart; it comes only from the clever mind which says, "I have read in books and I have heard from the Master that if I do not want anything from God, then God will give me everything." It is better to pray to God to give you peace of mind so that you can see the Truth in totality. To ask God for peace of mind is not a crime. If you do not have peace of mind, wherever you are, whether in the subway, in the country or in Times Square, there will be no God there for you. God has given us some intelligence. In the morning if you say, "God, it is up to You whether I eat or not. I will just stay here in bed," God is not going to put food into your mouth. No, God has given you the necessary intelligence to know that you have to put forth some effort. You have to leave the bed and take a shower and eat by your own effort.

In the inner life, if you want purity, humility, peace of mind and other divine qualities, then you have to make an effort to get them. It is true that if you do not pray to God for anything, then He will give you everything, but this truth has to be understood in its highest sense. If you do not pray to God or aspire for God-realisation or even think of God, then how do you expect God to give you everything? He will give you everything on the strength of your absolute faith in Him combined with your sincere inner cry.

The Upanishads come from the Vedas. What is the difference between the gifts which we get from the Vedas and the gifts which we get from the Upanishads? The Vedas are like a storehouse—everything is there, but it is not kept in proper order. Also, in it there are quite a few things which are unimportant for the modern world, for present-day life, for evolved human beings, for the intelligent or developed mind. The Upanishads come to our rescue. They take the inspiration and aspiration from the Vedas, but they have their own originality. All that is good in the Vedas the Upanishads gladly take and offer in a special manner.

Without the Vedas, the Upanishads do not exist. The Vedas are the source. But the wealth of the Vedas can be offered properly to the generality of mankind only through the Upanishads. The Upanishads have the capacity to enter into the source and offer the illumining, fulfilling wealth of the source in a way that can be accepted and understood by humanity at large. They are the end or cream of the Vedas; they are called Vedānta. On the mental plane, on the spiritual plane, on the psychic* plane, on the moral plane, all of India's achievements come from the polished, developed, aspiring and illumining consciousness of the Upanishads.

---

*Sri Chinmoy usually uses 'psychic' to refer to the spiritual heart.

Buddhism is a form of Vedānta philosophy. But the Buddha's philosophy emphasises a special aspect of Vedānta. We speak of the Buddha as the Lord of Compassion. We speak of the Buddha's ethics. Where did all this come from? From Vedānta. But while expressing the Vedāntic or Upanishadic truth, the Buddha offered his own inner light in a specific way. That is why ordinary human beings find it difficult to believe that Vedānta was the original source of the Buddha's teachings.

In the Western world we have Pythagoras and Plato, two great philosophers. You can see that the philosophy of both of them, especially Plato, has been greatly inspired by Upanishadic thought. Sufism, the emotional or psychic mysticism of the West, also comes from the same source, the Upanishads.

The world has received many significant things from the Upanishads, but unfortunately the world does not want to offer credit to the source. No harm. A child takes money from his parents and tells his friends that it is his money. Friends of his age believe that it is his, but adults will say, "He does not work. Where can he get money?" They know that he has received it from his parents. Millions of people have been inspired by the Upanishadic lore, consciously or unconsciously. In India and in the West there are many paths, many religions, which have taken abundant light from the Upanishads, but they find it hard to give credit to the source.

The Upanishadic seers abide within us. They do not need any appreciation or recognition. What do they want? What do they expect? From the genuine seekers of Truth, what they want and expect is the application of the Truth which has been offered. If the Truth is applied in our daily lives, no matter where it came from, divinity will loom large in us, and divinity will offer appreciation, admiration and glorification to the Source. Even God does not expect or demand anything more from us as long as we apply the Truth in our own lives consciously, constantly, devotedly, soulfully and unconditionally.

University of Connecticut
Storrs, Connecticut

Flame-Waves from the Upanishad-Sea, Part I

I

Aum bhūr bhuvaḥ svaḥ
Tat savitur vareṇyam
Bhargo devasya dhīmahi
Dhiyo yo naḥ pracodayāt (*Ṛgveda* III.62.10)

We meditate on the transcendental Glory of the Deity Supreme, who is inside the heart of the earth, inside the life of the sky and inside the soul of the Heaven. May He stimulate and illumine our minds.

Commentary

Illumination needed; here is the answer. Transcendental illumination transforms the animal in us, liberates the human in us, and manifests the Divine in us.

II

Pūrṇam adaḥ pūrṇam idaṃ pūrṇāt pūrṇam
udacyate
Pūrṇasya pūrṇam ādāya pūrṇam evāvaśiṣyate
(Invocation from the *Īśopaniṣad* and
Bṛhadāraṇyakopaniṣad)

Infinity is that. Infinity is this.
From Infinity, Infinity has come into
existence.
From Infinity, when Infinity is taken
away, Infinity remains.

Commentary

Infinity is the concealed Breath of the Pilot Supreme. Infinity is the revealed Life of the Supreme's Boat. Infinity is the fulfilled Body of the Goal supreme.

III

Asato mā sad gamaya
Tamaso mā jyotir gamaya
Mṛtyor māmṛtaṃ gamaya
(*Bṛhadāraṇyakopaniṣad* I.3.28)

Lead me from the unreal to the Real.
Lead me from darkness to Light.
Lead me from death to Immortality.

Commentary

The unreal in us desires the pleasure-life of the finite. The Real in us aspires for the God-Life of the Infinite.

Darkness is the discovery of the doubting and frustrated mind. Light is the discovery of the aspiring and dedicated heart.

Death—where is the cat? Miaowing nowhere. Immortality—where is the lion? Roaring all-where.

IV

Aṇor aṇīyān mahato mahīyān
Ātmāsya jantor nihito guhāyām
(*Kaṭhopaniṣad* 1.2.20)

Smaller than the smallest life, larger than
the infinite Vast,
The soul breathes in the secret heart of
man.

Commentary

The soul is God's eternal child and man's great-grandfather. As God's eternal child, the soul unceasingly plays. As man's great-grandfather, the soul perpetually enjoys rest.

V

Vedāham etaṃ puruṣaṃ mahāntam
Ādityavarṇam tamasaḥ parastāt
(*Śvetāśvataropaniṣad* 3.8; also *Yajurveda, Vājasaneyisaṃhitā* 31.18)

I have known this Great Being, effulgent as the sun, beyond the boundaries of tenebrous gloom.

Commentary

Before our realisation, this Great Being quenched our heart's thirst.

After our realisation, we feed the soul's hunger of this Great Being.

VI

Satyam eva jayate
(*Muṇḍakopaniṣad* 3.1.6)

Truth alone triumphs.

Commentary

Truth is God's Crown offered to God by God Himself.

Truth realised, God is forever caught.

VII

Devebhyaḥ kam āvṛṇīta mṛtyuṃ
Prajāyai kam amṛtaṃ nāvṛṇīta
(*Ṛgveda* X.13.4)

For the sake of the gods, he (Bṛhaspati) chose death.
He chose not Immortality for the sake of man.

Commentary

Bṛhaspati houses the flowing life of the gods and treasures the glowing love of man.

VIII

Uru ṇas tanve tan
Uru kṣayāya nas kṛdhi
Uru ṇo yaṃdhi jīvase (*Ṛgveda* VIII.68.12)

For our body give us freedom.
For our dwelling give us freedom.
For our life give us freedom.

Commentary

God's Compassion is the freedom of our body.
God's Concern is the freedom of our dwelling.
God's Love is the freedom of our life.

IX

Agnir jyotir jyotir agnir
Indro jyotir jyotir indraḥ
Sūryo jyotir jyotiḥ sūryaḥ
(*e.g. Sāmaveda* II.1181; *Yajurveda, Kāṭhakam* 40.6)

Agni is Light and the Light is Agni.
Indra is Light and the Light is Indra.
Sūrya is Light and the Light is Sūrya.

Commentary

Light is Love revealed.
Light is Life manifested.
Light is God fulfilled.

X

Ānandāddhyeva khalvimāni bhūtāni jāyante
Ānandena jātāni jīvanti
Ānandaṃ prayantyabhisaṃviśanti
(*Taittirīyopaniṣad* III.6)

From Delight we came into existence.
In Delight we grow.
At the end of our journey's close, into
Delight we retire.

Commentary

God has written an open letter to His human children. His letter runs: "My sweetest children, you are the only delight of My universal Existence."

XI

Hiraṇmayena pātreṇa satyasyāpihitaṃ mukham
Tat tvaṃ pūṣan apāvṛṇu satyadharmāya dṛṣṭaye
(*Bṛhadāraṇyakopaniṣad* V.15.1; also *Īśopaniṣad* 15)

The Face of Truth is covered with a brilliant golden orb. Remove it, O Sun, so that I who am devoted to the Truth may behold the Truth.

Commentary

The Face of Truth awakens us.
The Eye of Truth feeds us.
The Heart of Truth builds us.

XII

Saha nāvavatu saha nau bhunaktu
Saha vīryaṃ karavāvahai
(Invocation from the *Kaṭhopaniṣad;* also from parts 2 and 3 of the *Taittirīyopaniṣad*)

May He protect us together.
May He own us together.
May He make unto us vigour and virility.

Commentary

God, Guru and disciple: God is Compassion and Protection; Guru is concern; the disciple is dedication. When these three work together, perfect Perfection shines, and it will shine through Eternity.

XIII

Yenāhaṃ nāmṛtā syāṃ
Kim ahaṃ tena kuryām
(*Bṛhadāraṇyakopaniṣad* II.4.3)

What shall I do with the things that cannot make me immortal?

Commentary

God is eternally proud of man because he embodies God's Immortality.

XIV

Madhuman me parāyaṇam
Madhumat punarāyaṇam
(*Ṛgveda* X.24.6)

Sweet be my departure from home.
Sweet be my return.

Commentary

My sweet departure from my eternal home has made me feel how brave I am. My sweet return to my eternal home shall make me feel how fortunate I am.

Rutgers University
New Brunswick, New Jersey
18 February 1972

Flame-Waves from the Upanishad-Sea, Part II

I

Agne naya supathā rāye asmān
Viśvāni deva vayunāni vidvān
Yuyodhyasmaj juhurāṇam eno
Bhūyiṣṭhāṃ te namaüktiṃ vidhema
(*Ṛgveda* I.189.1; also *Īśopaniṣad* 18 and *Bṛhadāraṇyakopaniṣad* I.188.1, V.15.1)

O Agni, O Fire God, lead us along the right path so that we can enjoy the fruits of our divine actions. You know, O God, all our deeds. O God, take away from us all our unaspiring and binding sins and destroy them. To You we offer our teeming soulful salutations and prayers.

Commentary

Heart's aspiration is the right path. God's Compassion is the genuine guidance. The fruits of our divine actions are peace, light and bliss. Sin is the smile of self-limiting bondage. In our prayers and salutations abides God the illumining Saviour.

II

Uttiṣṭhata jāgrata prāpya varān nibodhata
Kṣurasya dhārā niśitā duratyayā
Durgaṃ pathas tat kavayo vadanti
(*Kaṭhopaniṣad* 1.3.14)

Arise! Awake! Realise and achieve the Highest with the help of the illumining, guiding and fulfilling Masters. The path is as sharp as the edge of a razor, difficult to cross, hard to tread—so declare the wise sages.

Commentary

"Arise! You need God. Awake! God needs you." Who brings this message? The Master. The road may be long, but not endless. The goal is not only an endless life, but an ever-energising, immortal breath. A wise sage is he whose outer life is the manifestation of the Truth's inner life.

III

Yo vai bhūmā tat sukhaṃ
Nālpe sukham asti
Bhūmaiva sukhaṃ
(*Chāndogyopaniṣad* VII.23.1)

The Infinite is the satisfying happiness.
In the finite no happiness can ever breathe.
The Infinite alone is the fulfilling happiness.

Commentary

The Life infinite is the Delight infinite.

The finite is a stranger to the infinite Happiness.

Infinity without Delight means the creation without a Creator. Indeed, this is absurd.

Delight without Infinity means the Creator without the creation. Indeed, this is equally absurd.

IV

Na tatra sūryo bhāti na candratārakaṃ
Nemā vidyuto bhānti kuto 'yam agniḥ
Tam eva bhāntam anubhāti sarvaṃ
Tasya bhāsā sarvam idaṃ vibhāti
(*Muṇḍakopaniṣad* 2.2.10 and
Śvetāśvataropaniṣad 6.14)

There the sun shines not, nor the moon and the stars, nor the lightning, let alone this earthly fire.

Only when illumining Light shines, everything else shines; the self-revealing Light illumines the entire universe.

Commentary

The outer sun asks us to see, and when we look around we see all darkness.

The inner sun makes us see what we eternally are: the Light infinite.

V

Nāyam ātmā balahīnena labhyo
(*Muṇḍakopaniṣad* 3.2.4)

The soul cannot be won by the weakling.

Commentary

True, a weak aspirant cannot realise his soul. Again, who can really be strong before he has realised his soul? A weak aspirant is God in His perfecting aspiration. A strong aspirant is God in His manifesting realisation.

VI

Yo devo agnau yo'psu viśvaṃ bhuvanam āviveśa
Ya oṣadhīṣu yo vanaspatiṣu tasmai devāya namo namaḥ
(*Śvetāśvataropaniṣad* 2.17)

We offer our supreme salutations to this divine Being, who is in fire, in water, in the plants, in the trees, and who has entered and pervaded the whole universe.

Commentary

Fire is aspiration.
Water is consciousness.
A plant is a climbing hope.
A tree is an assuring confidence.
The divine Being is the concealed Breath
and revealed Life of the universe.

VII

Vidyāñ cāvidyāñ ca yas tad vedobhayam saha
Avidyayā mṛtyuṃ tīrtvā vidyayāmṛtam aśnute
(*Īśopaniṣad* 11)

He who knows and understands knowledge and ignorance as one, through ignorance passes beyond the domain of death, through knowledge attains to an eternal Life and drinks deep the Light of Immortality.

Commentary

Ignorance is the knowledge of the physical mind. Knowledge is the secret of the soul. When the physical mind surrenders its existence to the illumination of the soul, death dies; Immortality dawns.

VIII

Bhadraṃ karṇebhiḥ śṛṇuyāma devā
Bhadraṃ paśyemākṣabhir yajatrāḥ
Sthirair aṅgais tuṣṭuvāṁsas tanūbhir
Vyaśema devahitaṃ yad āyuḥ
(Invocation from the *Muṇḍaka-, Praśna-* and *Māṇḍūkyopaniṣad;* originally from *Ṛgveda* I.89.8)

O cosmic gods, may we hear with our human ears all that is auspicious.

O gods who are truly worthy of worship, may we see with our human eyes all that is auspicious.

May we enjoy our life given by you, offering constant praises with our sound body and earthly existence to you.

Commentary

To hear an auspicious thing is to invoke God the Inspiration and God the Aspiration. To see an auspicious thing is to feel God the Light and God the Delight.

Fordham University
Bronx, New York

The Philosophy, Religion, Spirituality and Yoga of the Upanishads

The philosophy of the Upanishads is the vastness of the mind.

The religion of the Upanishads is the oneness of the heart.

The spirituality of the Upanishads is the Immortality of the soul.

The yoga of the Upanishads is the total manifestation of God here on earth.

The vastness of the mind needs God the infinite Consciousness.

The oneness of the heart needs God the supreme and eternal Beloved.

The Immortality of the soul needs God the ever-transcending Beyond.

The total manifestation of God needs man's constant inner hunger.

God is Purity in the vastness of the mind.
God is Beauty in the oneness of the heart.
God is Life in the Immortality of the soul.

The philosophy of the Upanishads tells me, "See the Truth."

The religion of the Upanishads tells me, "Feel the Truth."

The spirituality of the Upanishads tells me, "Grow into the Truth."

The yoga of the Upanishads tells me, "Become the Truth."

God tells me, "You are the Truth."

When I see the Truth, I know what God's Compassion is.

When I feel the Truth, I know what God's Love is.

When I grow into the Truth, I know what God's Concern is.

When I become the Truth, I know what God's selfless Life is, and what His unconditional Duty is.

When I realise that I am the Truth, the full manifestation of Divinity's Light begins.

The Upanishads offer to each aspiring heart countless messages. There are quite a few messages which are at once most significant and most fulfilling. Here is a stupendous message about life and death. Before death and after death, what happens? This is the message of the Upanishads:

Before death, life is a seeker.
After death, the same life becomes a dreamer.

Before death, life struggles and strives for perfection.

After death, the same life rests and enjoys the divine bliss with the soul.

Before death, life is God's Promise.

After death, life is God's inner Assurance. This Assurance of God's we notice while we fulfil God in our future incarnation.

Life for each individual is an act of inspiration and revelation. Life is an experience; even so is death. Our human life is God's sacred flame mounting towards the highest Source. Human death, the so-called death, is a secret play of God's Will.

When we study the Upanishads, we start with the concentration of the mind. This concentration of the mind is the most difficult thing that we can ever think of. We know what the mind is, we know what concentration is, but when it is a matter of concentration of the mind, it is extremely difficult to do.

Once some spiritual aspirants went to their Master and said, "Master, we have been meditating for so many years—for ten long years. How is it that we cannot control our minds?" The Master said, "My children, God-realisation is not so easy. Had it been easy, you would have by this time controlled your minds. God-realisation is extremely difficult—here is the proof. We consider the mind to be our developed part in our human life. But look at its helplessness." Then he went on to say, "You are all standing before me. Now if somebody stands up right on the shoulders of one of your spiritual brothers, what will happen? Immediately your brother will be irritated, he will feel disturbed. His prestige will be hurt. He is also a human being. How does someone dare to stand on his shoulders? The same thing happens to the mind. When the mind is agitated by our thoughts—low, undivine, uncomely thoughts—it does not allow us to become calm, quiet and serene enough to meditate on God."

The origin of the mind is divine; the mind itself is divine. But unfortunately the mind that we are using right now is the physical mind, which cannot help us at all in our upward journey. This mind has consciously or unconsciously accepted three undivine friends: fear, doubt and jealousy. I said in the beginning of this talk that the vastness of the mind is the philosophy of the Upanishads. When vastness wants to appear before the physical mind, the physical mind is horror-struck. It is afraid of the vastness. Further, it looks at its own insufficiency, its own limited capacity, and says, "How is it possible? I am so weak; I am so impotent; I am so insignificant. How can the vastness accept me as its very own?" First it is afraid of vastness. Then it doubts the very existence of vastness. Then, by God's infinite Grace, fear leaves the mind and doubt leaves the mind. Alas, now jealousy comes in. The mind looks around and sees that there is some fulfilment in the vastness, whereas in its own existence there is no fulfilment, there is no joy. Jealousy starts. Fear, doubt and jealousy—these three undivine forces attack the mind and make it meaningless, helpless and hopeless in our upward journey. When the mind is attacked by fear, doubt and jealousy, something else consciously and deliberately enters and feeds the mind, and that is our ego. With ego starts our spiritual end.

We have to go beyond the domain of the physical mind with the help of philosophy, religion, spirituality and yoga. The seeking mind operates in philosophy. The crying heart operates in religion. The illumining soul operates in spirituality. The fulfilling Goal operates in yoga.

There are two approaches to the Goal. One approach is through the mind; the other is through the heart. The approach of the mind is not safe; it is not secure. But one eventually can reach the Goal. It is not that if you approach God through the mind you will not realise God. You *will* realise God, but the road is arduous. You may doubt your aspiration; you may doubt God's Compassion for you. Hence it may take you hundreds, thousands of years to reach the Goal. But the approach through the heart is safe and sure. We can do one of two things: either we can identify ourselves with the Supreme Pilot, the Eternal Beloved, or we can surrender our existence at every second to the Inner Pilot. Either we have to become totally one with the Will of the Inner Pilot, or we have to surrender totally, unconditionally to the Inner Pilot. When we approach God in either of these ways, His Infinity, Eternity, Divinity and Immortality we feel immediately as our very own.

If we follow the messages of the Upanishads step by step, if we start first with philosophy, then with religion, then with spirituality and finally with yoga, then God-realisation need not and cannot remain a far cry. God-discovery is our birthright. If we really want to discover God, then we can start right from the beginning: philosophy, religion, spirituality and yoga. When we fulfil the demands of philosophy, religion, spirituality and yoga, God fulfils all our demands. Their demands are very simple: aspiration and self-control. Our demands are God's gifts: peace, light, bliss and power.

Do we really care for God's gifts? If we really care for God's gifts, then God will offer us the capacity to receive His infinite wealth. In our ordinary life when we want something from somebody else, that person will not give us the capacity to receive it. He will demand our own capacity. If we have the capacity, if we work for one day, then the boss will give us the salary. But in the spiritual life, God wants to know whether we really want the salary—peace, light and bliss. If we want them, then He Himself will energise us and be our aspiration and self-control. He will work in and through us. He will work as the seeker within us, and at the same time He will work as the Pilot for us. He Himself will be both Employer and employee. If we really want God, God will play at once both the roles. He will be the Giver and the receiver. He will be the seeker and the Fulfiller.

University of Massachusetts
Amherst, Massachusetts

Commentary on the Bhagavad Gita

The Song of the Transcendental Soul

Introduction

I read the Gita because it is the Eye of God. I sing the Gita because it is the Life of God. I live the Gita because it is the Soul of God.

The Gita is God's Vision immediate. The Gita is God's Reality direct.

They say that the Gita is a Hindu book, a most significant scripture. I say that it is the Light of Divinity in humanity. They say that the Gita needs an introduction. I say that God truly wants to be introduced by the Gita.

Arjuna is the ascending human soul. Krishna is the descending divine Soul. Finally they meet. The human soul says to the divine Soul: "I need You." The divine Soul says to the human soul: "I need you, too. I need you for My self-manifestation. You need Me for your self-realisation." Arjuna says: "O Krishna, You are mine, absolutely mine." Krishna says: "O Arjuna, no mine, no thine. We are the oneness complete, within, without."

The Gita is an episode in the sixth book of the Mahābhārata. *Mahābhārata* means 'Great India', 'India the Sublime'. This unparalleled epic is six times the size of the Iliad and the Odyssey combined. Surprising in size and amazing in thought is the Mahābhārata. The main story revolves around a giant rivalry between two parties of cousins. Their ancestral kingdom was the apple of discord. This rivalry came to its close at the end of a great battle called the Battle of Kurukṣetra.

Sāntanu had two wives: Gaṅgā and Satyavatī. Bhīṣma was born from the union of Sāntanu and Gaṅgā; Citrāṅgada and Vicitravīrya from that of Sāntanu and Satyavatī. Vicitravīrya's two wives were Ambikā and Ambālikā. Dhṛtarāṣṭra was the son of Ambikā and Vicitravīrya; Pāṇḍu, the son of Ambālikā and Vicitravīrya. Dhṛtarāṣṭra's hundred sons were the Kauravas; Pāṇḍu's five sons, the Pāṇḍavas.

Yudhiṣṭhira was the legitimate heir to the kingdom. His father, Pāṇḍu, had reigned a number of years, offering the utmost satisfaction to his subjects. Finally Pāṇḍu retired to the forest. To succeed him was his eldest son, Yudhiṣṭhira, and he did it devotedly and successfully. Dhṛtarāṣṭra was Pāṇḍu's elder half brother. God had denied him sight. Strangely enough, his affection for his hundred sons blinded his heart as well. Being blind, naturally he was not qualified to inherit the throne. The eldest son of Dhṛtarāṣṭra was Duryodhana. Ninety-nine brothers were to follow him. Yudhiṣṭhira, Pāṇḍu's eldest son, had only four brothers to follow him.

Truth's pride was Yudhiṣṭhira. Falsehood's pride was Duryodhana. Through the illumined hearts of Pāṇḍu's five sons, God smiled. Through the unlit minds of Dhṛtarāṣṭra's hundred sons, the devil smiled. The devil often succeeded in embracing the blind father, too.

The eyeless father made repeated requests, strong and weak, to Duryodhana, his morally, psychically and spiritually eyeless son, not to go to war. Vidura, the pure heart, Duryodhana's uncle, failed to throw light on Duryodhana's thick head. Sañjaya, his father's prudent charioteer, equally failed. Neither was Bhīṣma, the oldest and the wisest, successful. Duryodhana felt his own understanding to be superior. Finally Sri Krishna, the Lord of the universe, most fervently tried to avert the hurtful and heartless battle. But the ignorance-night in Duryodhana would by no means surrender to the knowledge-sun in Sri Krishna.

Seven hundred verses are there in the Gita. About six hundred are the soul-stirring utterances from the divine lips of Lord Krishna, and the rest are from the crying, aspiring Arjuna, the clairvoyant and clairaudient Sañjaya, and the inquisitive Dhṛtarāṣṭra.

The sage Vyāsa enquired of Dhṛtarāṣṭra if he desired to see the events and have a first-hand knowledge of the battle, from the battle's birth to the battle's death. The sage was more than willing to grant the blind man vision. But Dhṛtarāṣṭra did not want his eyes—the eyes that had failed him all his life—to obey his command at this terribly fateful hour for his conscience and his kingdom's life, especially when his own sons were heading for destruction. He declined the sage's kind and bounteous offer. His heart was ruthlessly tortured by the imminent peril of his kinsmen. However, he requested the sage to grant the boon to someone else from whom he could get faultless reports of the battle. Vyāsa consented. He conferred upon Sañjaya the miraculous psychic power of vision to see the incidents taking place at a strikingly great distance.

Is the Gita a mere word? No. A speech? No. A concept? No. A kind of concentration? No. A form of meditation? No. What is it, then? It is *The Realisation*. The Gita is God's Heart and man's breath, God's Assurance and man's promise.

The inspiration of Hinduism is the soul-concern of the Gita. The aspiration of Hinduism is the blessing-dawn of the Gita. The emancipation of Hinduism is the compassion-light of the Gita. But to pronounce that the Gita is the sole monopoly of Hinduism is absurdity. The Gita is the common property of humanity.

The West says that she has something special to offer to the East: the New Testament. The East accepts the offer with deepest gratitude and offers her greatest pride, the Bhagavad Gita, in return.

The Gita is unique. It is the Scripture of scriptures. Why? Because it has taught the world that the emotion pure, the devotion genuine can easily run abreast with the philosophy solid, the detachment dynamic.

There are eighteen chapters in the Gita. Each chapter reveals a specific teaching of a particular form of Yoga. Yoga is the secret language of man and God. *Yoga* means 'union', the union of the finite with the Infinite, the union of the form with the Formless. It is Yoga that reveals the supreme secret: man is tomorrow's God and God is today's man. Yoga is to be practised for the sake of Truth. If not, the seeker will be sadly disappointed. Likewise, man's God-realisation is for the sake of God. Otherwise untold frustration will be man's inevitable reward.

The Gita was born in 600 B.C. Its authorship goes to the sage Vedavyāsa. With a significant question from Dhṛtarāṣṭra, the Gita commences its journey. The whole narrative of the Bhagavad Gita is Sañjaya's answer to Dhṛtarāṣṭra's single question. Sri Krishna spoke much—all divinely soulful. Arjuna spoke little—all humanly heartful. Dhṛtarāṣṭra was the listener. The divinely and humanly clairvoyant and clairaudient reporter was Sañjaya. On very rare occasions Sañjaya contributed his own thoughtful remarks too.

Sri Krishna was Arjuna's body's relation, heart's union and soul's liberation. As God, He illumined

Arjuna with the Truth absolute; as a humane human, he illumined his earthly friend with truths relative.

Philosophers enter into a deplorable controversy. Some enquire how such a philosophical discourse could take place at the commencement of a war. How was it possible? There are others who firmly hold that this momentous discourse was not only possible but inevitable at that hour, since it was the divinely appropriate occasion for the aspiring Hindu to discover the inner meaning of war and live in accordance with his soul's dictates, instead of following the poor, unlit knowledge of morality.

The Gita is the epitome of the Vedas. It is spontaneous. It is in a form at once divinised and humanised. It is also the purest milk drawn from the udders of the most illumining Upanishads to feed and nourish the human soul. The Gita demands man's acceptance of life and reveals the way to achieve the victory of the higher Self over the lower self by the spiritual art of transformation: physical, vital, mental, psychic and spiritual.

The Gita embodies the soul-wisdom, the heart-love, the mind-knowledge, the vital-dynamism and the body-action.

The Sorrow of Arjuna

The Gita begins with the words *Dharmakṣetre Kurukṣetre* (*Bhagavad Gītā* 1.1). 'On the hallowed field of Kurukṣetra'—this is the literal translation. *Kṣetra* means 'field'. *Dharma* is a spiritual word, and it is extremely fertile in meanings. It means the inner code of life; moral, religious and spiritual law; living faith in God's existence and in one's own existence; soulful duty, especially enjoined by the scriptures; devoted observances of any caste or sect; willingness to abide by the dictates of one's soul.

The Sanskrit root of the word *dharma* is *dhṛ*, 'to hold'. Who holds us? God. What holds us? Truth. Dharma prevails. If not always, ultimately it must, for in dharma is the very Breath of God.

Duryodhana went to Gāndhārī, his mother, on the eve of the war, for her benediction. Like mother, like son. Here is a veritable exception. She blessed Duryodhana saying, "Victory will be there, where dharma is." It meant that Yudhiṣṭhira, the son of dharma, would win the war. She was the possessor of such a selfless heart. Something more: the present world observes her unique dharma in her unparalleled acceptance of her husband's fate. God gave Dhṛtarāṣṭra no sight. Gāndhārī proved her absolute oneness with her blind husband by binding her own eyes. She embraced blindness—a sacrifice worthy to be remembered and admired by humanity. She saw not the world without. The choice blessings of the world within showered on Gāndhārī.

Our body's dharma is service, our mind's dharma is illumination, our heart's dharma is oneness and our soul's dharma is liberation.

Again, people are apt to claim that dharma means religion. If so, how many religions are there? Just one. Certainly not two, not to speak of three. And what does religion signify? It signifies man-discovery and God-discovery, which are one and identical.

Now let us focus our attention on the word *dharmakṣetra*, 'the field of dharma'. Why is Kurukṣetra called *'dharmakṣetra'*? A battlefield can be anything but *dharmakṣetra*, but this battle took place on Kurukṣetra where untold religious sacrifices were performed. And something more. Kurukṣetra was situated between two sacred rivers—the Yamuna and the Saraswati in the northwestern part of India. A river is perpetually sacred. A river houses water. Water signifies consciousness in the domain of spirituality, and this consciousness is always pure, unalloyed, sanctifying and energising. So we now come to learn why Kurukṣetra was called '*dharmakṣetra*' and not otherwise.

To consider the first chapter as an introductory chapter and pay very little importance to it, as some scholars, interpreters and readers do, need not be an act of wisdom. The first chapter has a special significance of its own. It deals with Arjuna's sorrow, his inner conflict. Poor Arjuna was torn with grief between two equally formidable ideas: he must go to war or he must not. Curiously enough, Arjuna's mother, Kuntī Devī, prayed to the Lord Krishna to bless her with perpetual sorrow. Why? Kuntī Devī realised that if sorrow deserted her for good, surely there would be no necessity on her part to invoke Sri Krishna. Her world always wanted sorrow, suffering and tribulation, so that her heart could treasure constantly the Lord's all-compassionate Presence. To a degree, we can recall in the same vein, from Keats' "Endymion":

> But cheerly, cheerly she [sorrow] loves me
>   dearly;
> She is so constant to me, and so kind.

Actually, from the highest spiritual point of view, we cannot welcome Kuntī Devī's wisdom. Nevertheless, it served her purpose most effectively. A spiritual person has not to embrace sorrow with the hope of achieving God's Bounty. He has to aspire. His aspiration has to reveal God's Presence within him—God's Love, Peace, Bliss and Power. He takes sorrow as an experience in his life. He also knows that it is God who is having this experience in him and through him.

True, sorrow purifies our emotional heart. But the divine Light performs this task infinitely more successfully. Yet one has not to be afraid of sorrow's arrival in one's life. Far from it. Sorrow has to be transformed into joy everlasting. How? With our heart's mounting aspiration and God's ever-flowing Compassion combined. Why? Because God is all Joy, and what we humans want is to see, feel, realise and eventually become God, the Blissful.

The principal warriors were now seen on both sides. Some were eager to fight in order to display their mighty valour, while there were matchless warriors like Bhīṣma, Droṇa and Kṛpa who fought out of moral obligation. On the battlefield itself, just before the actual battle took place, Yudhiṣṭhira walked barefoot to the opposing army, precisely to Bhīṣma and Droṇa and other well-wishers, for their benedictions. Bhīṣma, while blessing Yudhiṣṭhira from the inmost recesses of his heart, said, "Son, my body will fight, while my heart will be with you and your brothers. Yours is the victory destined." Droṇa, while blessing Yudhiṣṭhira, exclaimed, "I am a victim to obligation. I shall fight for the Kauravas, true. But yours will be the victory. This is the assurance from my Brahmin heart."*

Blessings over, Yudhiṣṭhira returned. There blared forth countless trumpets, conches, wardrums and bugles. Elephants trumpeted, horses neighed. The wildest tempest broke loose.

Arrows flew like meteors in the air. Forgotten was the sweet, old affection. Broken were the ties of blood. Death was singing the song of death. Here we may recall Tennyson's "The Charge of the Light Brigade":

> Cannon to right of them,
> Cannon to left of them,
> Cannon in front of them
> Volley'd and thunder'd;
> Storm'd at with shot and shell,
> Boldly they rode and well
> Into the jaws of Death,
> Into the mouth of hell
> Rode the six hundred.

The cannon had not been invented in the days of the Mahābhārata, but the scene of death was the same, with arrows, swords, maces and missiles. Needless to say, we must identify ourselves with the arrows, maces and lion-roars of the Kurukṣetra

---

*Cf. *Mahābhārata* VI.41; *The Mahabharata,* V.S. Suktankar and S.K. Belvalkar, ed., Poona, 1933–1959.

heroes and not with today's grandiose war-achievements. The joy of knowing the achievements of the hoary past is at once irresistible and unfathomable.

Arjuna exclaimed, "Pray, place my chariot, O Krishna, between the two battle formations so that I can see those who thirst for war (1.21-22)." He surveyed the battle scene. Alas, he saw among the deadly opponents those very human souls whom he had always held dear and near. Overwhelmed with tenebrous grief, Arjuna, for the first time in his life of matchless heroism, gave unthinkable expression to faint-heartedness. "My body shivers, my mouth is parched, my limbs give way, fear tortures me all over, my hair stands on end, my bow slips from my hand and my mind is reeling. Hard is it even for me to stand. Krishna, victory over them, my present foes, I seek not. They were my own. Still they are. Neither kingdom nor ease I seek. Let them attack; they want to and they shall. But I shall not hurl my weapon upon them, not even for the supreme sovereignty of the three worlds, let alone the earth!" (1.29-35)

With one moral weapon after another, Arjuna attacked Sri Krishna. He was determined to discard his war weapons for good. He started his philosophy with the correct anticipation of the slaughter of his kinsmen, the dire calamity of family destruction. He emphasised that virtue being lost, family would be caught tight in the grip of vice. This would all be due to lawlessness. When lawlessness predominates, the women of the family become corrupt; women corrupted, caste-confusion comes into existence.

A word about caste-confusion. India is still being mercilessly ridiculed for clinging to the caste system. In fact, caste is unity in diversity. Each caste is like a limb of the body. The four castes: Brahmin (the priest), Kshatriya (the warrior), Vaishya (the agriculturist) and Shudra (the labourer). The origin of the castes we observe in the Vedas. The Brahmin is the mouth of *Puruṣa*, the Supreme personified; Kshatriya, His two arms; Vaishya, His two thighs; Shudra, His two feet.

In connection with caste-destruction, Arjuna also tells Lord Krishna that everything is leading towards perilous sin. In the Western world, unfortunately, the word 'sin' seems to loom large in every walk of life. It is something more fatal than perdition. To Westerners, I beg to be excused, sin is part and parcel of life. In the East, especially in India, the word 'sin' offers a different meaning. It means imperfection, nothing more and nothing less. The human consciousness is proceeding from imperfection to perfection. The seers of the Upanishads gave no importance to sin. They taught the world the serenity, sanctity, integrity and divinity of man.

To come back to poor Arjuna, said he: "Let the sons of Dhṛtarāṣṭra, armed with weapons, end my life, while I am unarmed, with no resistance. I prefer in all sincerity my death to our victory!" (1.46)

Lo, Arjuna, the hero supreme! Discarding his bow and arrows, dolefully, throbbingly and soulfully he sinks into the rear of his chariot.

"Fighting is not for Arjuna. Krishna, I shall not fight."(cf. 2.9)

Knowledge

This chapter is entitled "*Sāṃkhya Yoga*"—"The Yoga of Knowledge." Arjuna's arguments against war are very plausible to our human understanding. Sri Krishna read Arjuna's heart. Confusion ran riot across Arjuna's mind. The unmanly sentiment in his Kshatriya blood he took as his love for mankind. Arjuna was never wanting in sincerity. His mouth spoke what his heart felt. Unfortunately his sincerity unconsciously housed ignorance. Krishna wanted to illumine Arjuna. "O Arjuna, in your speech, you are a philosopher; in your action, you are not. A true philosopher mourns neither for the living nor for the dead. But Arjuna, you are sorrowing and grieving. Tell me, why do you mourn the prospective death of these men? You existed, I existed, they too. Never shall we cease to exist." (2.11-12)

We have just mentioned Arjuna's philosophy. Truth to tell, we too would have fared the same at that juncture. Real philosophy is truly difficult to study, more difficult to learn, and most difficult to live.

The Sanskrit word for philosophy is *darśana*, meaning 'to see, to envision.' Sri Ramakrishna's significant remark runs: "In the past, people used to have visions *(darśana)*; now people study *darśana* (philosophy)!"

Equally significant is the message of the Hebrew Bible: "Your old men shall dream dreams; your young men shall see visions." (Joel 3:1)

Arjuna for the first time came to learn from Sri Krishna that his human belief concerning life and death was not founded on truth. He felt that he was distracted by illusions. He prayed to Sri Krishna for enlightenment: "I am your humble disciple. Teach me. Tell me what is best for me." (2.7) For the first time, the word 'disciple' sprang from Arjuna's lips.

Until then, Sri Krishna had been his friend and comrade. The disciple learned: "The Reality that pervades the universe is the Life immortal. The body is perishable; the soul, the real in man, or the real man, is deathless, immortal. The soul neither kills nor is killed. Beyond birth and death, constant and eternal is the soul. The knower of this truth neither slays nor causes slaughter." (2.17-21)

Arjuna had to fight the battle of life and not the so-called Battle of Kurukṣetra. Strength he had. Wisdom he needed. The twilight consciousness of the physical mind he had. He needed the sun-bright consciousness of the soul's divinity.

Sri Krishna used the terms 'birth', 'life', and 'death'. Birth is the passing of the soul from a lower to a higher body in the process of evolution, in the course of the soul's journey of reincarnation. The *Sāṃkhya* system affirms the absolute identity of cause and effect. Cause is the effect silently and secretly involved and effect is the cause actively and openly evolved. Evolution, according to the *Sāṃkhya* philosophy, can never come into existence from nothing, from zero. The appearance of 'is' can be only from the existence of 'was'. Let us fill our minds with the immortal utterance of Wordsworth from "Intimations of Immortality":

> Our birth is but a sleep and a forgetting:
> The Soul that rises with us, our life's Star,
> Hath had elsewhere its setting,
> And cometh from afar:
> Not in entire forgetfulness,
> And not in utter nakedness,
> But trailing clouds of glory do we come
> From God who is our home.

Here the poet carries us into the mystery of the soul's eternal journey and reminds us of the perennial Source.

What is life? It is the soul's only opportunity to manifest and fulfil the Divine here on earth. When life begins its journey, Infinity shakes hands with it. When the journey is half done, Eternity shakes hands with it. When life's journey is complete, Immortality shakes hands with it. Life lives the life of perfection when it lives in spirituality. When life lives in spirituality, the Breath of God, it stands far above the commands of morality and the demands of duty.

God says to the human life, "Arise, awake, aspire! Yours is the goal." The human life says to God: "Wait, I am resting. I am sleeping. I am dreaming." Suddenly life feels ashamed of its conduct. Crying, it says, "Father, I am coming." Throbbing, it says, "Father, I am come." Smiling, it says, "Father, I have come."

Life, the problem, can be solved by the soul, the solution; but for that, one has first to be awakened from within.

He who lives the inner life knows that death is truly his resting room. To him, death is anything but extinction. It is a meaningful departure. When our consciousness is divinely transformed, the necessity of death will not arise at all. To transform life, we need peace, light, bliss and power. We cry for these divine qualities. They cry for our aspiration. They are equally anxious to grant us everlasting life. But until our body, vital, mind, heart and soul aspire together, the divine power, light, bliss and peace cannot possess us.

The body dies, but not the soul. The body sleeps; the soul flies. The soul-stirring words on death and the soul in this chapter of the Gita, let us recollect. "Even as a man discards old clothes for new ones, so the dweller in the body, the soul, leaving aside the worn-out bodies, enters into new bodies. The soul migrates from body to body. Weapons cannot cleave it, nor fire consume it, nor water drench it, nor wind dry it." (2.22–23) This is the soul and this is what is meant by the existence of the soul.

Now we shall be well advised to observe the existence of death, if there is any, in the momentous words of Sri Aurobindo, the founder of the Integral Yoga. "Death," he exclaims, "has no separate existence by itself. It is only a result of the principle of decay in the body and that principle is there already—it is part of the physical nature. At the same time it is not inevitable; if one could have the necessary consciousness and force, decay and death are not inevitable."*

What we call death is nothing short of ignorance. We can solve the problem of death only when we know what life is. Life is eternal. It existed before birth and it will exist after death. Life also exists between birth and death. It is beyond birth and death. Life is infinite. Life is immortal. A seeker of the infinite Truth cannot subscribe to

*Sri Aurobindo, *Letters on Yoga,* vol. 3, Pondicherry, 1971, p. 1230.

Schopenhauer's statement: "To desire immortality is to desire the eternal perpetuation of a great mistake." There is no shadow of doubt that it is the ceaseless seeker in man who is Immortality's life, for his very existence indicates the Supreme's Vision that illumines the universe and the Supreme's Reality that fulfils creation.

Arjuna the disciple further learned: "Do your duty. Do not waver. Be not faint-hearted. You are a Kshatriya. There can be no greater invitation than that of a righteous war for a Kshatriya." (2.31)

A Kshatriya's (warrior's) duty can never be the duty of an ascetic. Neither should an ascetic perform the duty of a Kshatriya. Also, a Kshatriya must not follow the path of a world-renouncer. Imitation is not for a seeker. "Imitation is suicide," so do we learn from Emerson.

A warrior's duty is to fight, fight for the establishment of Truth. "In his victory, the entire earth becomes his; in his death, him welcome the gates of Paradise." (2.37)

Sri Krishna unveiled the path of *sāṃkhya* (knowledge) to Arjuna: "Arjuna, take them as one, victory and defeat, joy and sorrow, gain and loss. Care not for them. Fight! Fighting thus, no sin will you incur." (2.38)

The Teacher revealed the path of knowledge *(sāṃkhya)*. Now he wanted to teach the student the path of action *(karma yoga)*. Arjuna surprisingly learned that this path, the path of action, the second path, is fruitful and also will bring him deliverance. The truth sublime is: "Action is your birthright, not the outcome, not the fruits thereof. Let not the fruits of action be your object, and be not attached to inaction. Be active and dynamic; seek not any reward." (2.47) We can simultaneously kindle the flame of our consciousness with the lore of the Īśā Upanishad: "Action cleaves not to a man." (*Īśopaniṣad* 2)

We have already used the term 'yoga'. What is yoga? "Equanimity," says Sri Krishna, "is yoga." (2.48) He also says: "Yoga is skilful wisdom in action." (2.50)

Arjuna's inner progress is striking. He now feels the necessity to free himself from the desire-life. Sri Krishna teaches him how he can totally detach himself from the bondage-life of the senses as a tortoise successfully withdraws its limbs from all directions. Sense-withdrawal, or withdrawal from the sense objects, by no means indicates the end of man's journey. "Mere withdrawal cannot put an end to desire's birth. Desire disappears only when the Supreme appears. In His Presence the desire-life loses its existence, not before." (2.59)

This second chapter throws considerable light on *sāṃkhya* (knowledge) and *yoga* (action). *Sāṃkhya* and *yoga* are never at daggers drawn. One is detached meditative knowledge, and the other is dedicated and selfless action. They have the self-same goal.

They just follow two different paths to arrive at the goal.

To come back to the sense-life, sense-life is not to be discontinued. Sense-life is to be lived in the Divine for the Divine. It is the inner withdrawal, not the outer withdrawal, that is imperative. The animal in man has to surrender to the Divine in man for its total transformation. The life of animal pleasure must lose its living and burning breath in the all-fulfilling life of divine bliss.

The Kaṭha Upanishad declares the rungs of the ever-climbing ladder:

> Higher than the senses are the objects of
> sense,
> Higher than the objects of sense is the
> mind,
> Higher than the mind is the intellect,
> Higher than the intellect is the Self,
> Higher than the Self is the Unmanifest,
> Higher than the Unmanifest is
> the Supreme personified,
> Highest is this Supreme,
> the Goal Ultimate.
>
> (*Kaṭhopaniṣad* 1.3.10-11)

We have seen what happens when we go up. Let us observe what happens when we muse on the sense-objects. The Gita tells us: "Dwelling on sense-objects gives birth to attachment; attachment gives birth to desire. Desire (unfulfilled) brings into existence the life of anger. From anger delusion springs up, from delusion the confusion of memory. In the confusion of memory the reasoning wisdom is lost. When wisdom is nowhere, destruction within, without, below and above." (2.62-63)

The dance of destruction is over. Let us pine for salvation. The disciplined, self-controlled aspirant alone will be blessed by the flood of peace. Finally, the aspirant will be embraced by salvation, the inner illumination.

Action

On the strength of our identification with Arjuna's heart, we are apt to feel, at the beginning of the third chapter, that we are thrown into the world of ruthless confusion and immense doubt. Arjuna wants immediate relief from his mental tension; he wants to hear a decisive truth. His impatience prevents him from seeing the total Truth in all its aspects. In the preceding chapter, his divine Teacher, Sri Krishna, expressed his deep appreciation for the path of knowledge, but at the same time, told Arjuna of the great necessity of action. The Teacher, needless to say, had not the slightest intention of throwing the student into the sea of confusion. Far from it. What Arjuna required was a broader vision of Truth and a deeper meaning of Reality. When we see through the eyes of Arjuna, we see that his world is a world of conflicting ideas. But when we see through the eyes of Sri Krishna, we see a world of complementary facets of the all-sustaining and all-pervading Truth.

Knowledge and action, Arjuna believed, would lead him to the same goal. Why then is he doomed or expected to wade through the bloodshed of war, enjoined by action?

True, Arjuna's mental sky was overcast with heavy clouds, but his psychic sky pined for true enlightenment. His mighty question is, "If you consider knowledge superior to action, why urge me to this dreadful action?" (3.1)

Sri Krishna now says, "Two paths, Arjuna, are there, as I have already told you—the path of knowledge and the path of action. Through the divine art of contemplation, the aspirant follows the path of knowledge. Through the dynamic urge of selfless work, the seeker follows the path of action." (3.3)

Knowledge feels that the world within is the real world. Action feels that the world without is the real world. The path of knowledge enters inside from outside, while the path of action enters outside from inside. This is the difference. But this apparent duality can never be the whole truth, the Truth ultimate.

There is an Arabian proverb which says:

> There are four sorts of men:
>
> He who knows not and knows not that he knows not: he is a fool—shun him;
> He who knows not and knows that he knows not: he is simple—teach him;
> He who knows and knows not that he knows: he is asleep—wake him;

He who knows and knows that he knows: he is wise—follow him.

Arjuna, too, had to go through these four stages of evolution. At the end of the first chapter, he declared, "O Krishna, I shall not fight."(2.9) He did not know what Truth was, yet he was ignorant of this fact. Krishna, being all Compassion, could not shun His dearest Arjuna.

"I pray, tell me what is best for me." (2.7) Here Arjuna's simple sincerity touches the depth of Sri Krishna's heart and the Teacher begins to instruct the aspirant.

Arjuna had known all his life that heroism was the very breath of a Kshatriya like himself, but his mind temporarily eclipsed this inner knowledge. He was in the world of deluding sleep. So Sri Krishna had to arouse him, saying, "Arjuna, fight! In victory, you will enjoy the sovereignty of the earth; in death, wide open are the gates of Paradise." (2.37)

Finally Arjuna realised that Sri Krishna not only knew the Truth but also was the Truth. So he wanted to follow Sri Krishna. He cried out, "*Śaraṇāgataḥ*—You are my refuge. I am at Your Command."

He who follows the path of action is by nature simple, says Krishna. He is simple; his action is direct; the result is immediate. Arjuna, however, wants freedom from action, which is nothing short of impossibility. Action is done not only by the body, but also in the body by the mind. Action plays its role also in the conscious and sub-conscious levels of one's being. Action cannot die. It can never dream of an escape so long as the impulses of nature are alive. Action binds us only when we bind action with our likes and dislikes. The action-tree grows within us either with its venomous or with its ambrosial fruits.

According to Shankara, one may doubt the existence of God, but it is impossible for one to doubt one's own existence. A human being, if he houses common sense, believes in his present existence. If he cares to go one step ahead, he has to accept the undeniable existence of destiny. And what is destiny? Destiny is the evolving experience of one's consciousness. This experience is neither obscure nor uncertain. It is the necessary inevitability of a cosmic law striving for its outer manifestation in perfect Perfection.

Action and reaction are the obverse and reverse of the same coin. At times they may appear to be two dire foes. Nevertheless, their equal capacity is undeniable. The Son of God made the lofty statement: "They that take the sword shall perish by the sword." (Matthew 26:52)

Action itself does not have a binding power; neither does it need one. It is the desire in action that has the power to bind us and tell us that freedom is not for mortals. But if, in action, sacrifice looms large, or if action is done in a spirit of sacrifice, or if action is considered another name for sacrifice, then action is perfection, action is illumination, action is liberation.

For him who is embodied, action is a necessity, action is a must. Man is the result of a divine sacrifice. It is sacrifice that can vision the truth and fulfil man's existence. In sacrifice alone we see the connecting and fulfilling link between one individual and another. No doubt the world is progressing and evolving. Yet, in the Western world sacrifice is often considered synonymous with stupidity and ignorance. To quote William Q. Judge, one of the early leading Theosophists:

> Although Moses established sacrifices for the Jews, the Christian successors have abolished it both in spirit and letter, with a curious inconsistency which permits them to ignore the words of Jesus that 'not one jot or tittle of the law should pass until all these things were fulfilled'.

To be sure, the East of today is no exception.

What is sacrifice? It is the discovery of universal oneness. In the Rig Veda we observe the supreme sacrifice made by the sage Bṛhaspati:

> *Devebhyaḥ kam āvṛṇīta mṛtyuṃ...*
> (*Ṛgveda* X.13.4)

For the sake of the gods, he chose death.
He chose not Immortality for the sake of man.

Sacrifice is the secret of self-dedicated service. It was fear or some other doubtful motive which compelled some primitive minds to embrace sacrifice. They thought that the eyes of the cosmic gods would emit fire if they did not sacrifice animals as an offering. At least they were wise enough not to sacrifice children, their nearest and dearest. The Supreme wanted and still wants and will always want sacrifice from both human beings and the gods for their reciprocal benefit. It is their mutual sacrifice that makes both the parties one and indivisible. Men will offer their aspiration; the gods will offer their illumination. A man of true satisfaction is a man of consecrated offering. Sin can stand nowhere near him. The existence of humanity as a whole demands attention first; the individual existence next. Work done in the spirit of purest offering leads an aspirant to the abode of perfect bliss.

Possession is not satisfaction, so long as ego breathes in us. The great King Janaka knew it. No wonder Janaka was loved by the sage Yājñavalkya most. His Brahmin disciples felt that Janaka received preference just because he was king. It is obvious that God would not let the sage Yājñavalkya suffer such foul criticism. What happened? Mithilā,

Janaka's capital, began to burn in mounting and devouring flames. The disciples ran, left their preceptor, hurried to their respective cottages. What for? Just to save their loin cloths. All fled save Janaka. He ignored his riches and treasures burning in the city. Janaka stayed with his Guru, Yājñavalkya, listening to the sage's ambrosial talk.

> *Mithilāyām pradagdhāyāṃ na me kiñcit praṇaśyati...**
>
> Nothing do I lose, even though Mithila may be consumed to ashes.

Now the disciples came to learn why their Guru favoured Janaka most. This is the difference between a man of wisdom and a man of ignorance. An ignorant man knows that what he has is the body. A man of wisdom knows that what he has and what he is, is the soul. Hence to him the soul's needs are of paramount importance.

Sri Krishna disclosed to Arjuna the secret of Janaka's attainment to self-realisation and salvation. Janaka acted with detachment. He acted for the sake of humanity, having been surcharged with the light and wisdom of Divinity. Indeed, this is the path of the noble. Krishna wanted Arjuna to tread this path,

---

*This seems to be a well-known utterance of King Janaka, quoted in slightly different form *(Mithilāyām pradagdhāyāṃ na me dahyati kiñcana)* in *Mahābhārata* XII.17.18.

so that the world would follow him. Perhaps Arjuna was not fully convinced. In order to convince Arjuna fully and unreservedly, Krishna gave the example of Himself: "Nothing have I to do in the three worlds, nor is there anything worth attaining, unattained by me; yet do I perpetually work, I ever have my existence in action. If I do not work, the worlds will perish." (3.22-24)

Sri Krishna wanted Arjuna to be freed from the fetters of ignorance. The only way Arjuna could do it was to act without attachment. Sri Krishna told Arjuna the supreme secret: "Dedicate all action to Me, with your mind fixed on Me, the Self in all." (3.30)

All beings must follow their nature. No escape there is, nor can there be. What can restraint do? Man's duty is Heaven's peerless blessing. One must know what one's duty is. Once duty is known, it is to be performed to the last.

> I slept and dreamed that life was Beauty;
> I woke and found that life was Duty.
>
> —*Ellen S. Hooper, "Duty"*

Life's duty, performed with a spontaneous flow of self-offering to humanity under the express guidance of the inner being, can alone transform life into beauty, the Heavenly beauty of the world within and earthly beauty of the world without.

Arjuna's duty was to fight, for he was a Kshatriya, a warrior. This fighting was not for power, but for the establishment of truth over falsehood. Sri Krishna's most encouraging and inspiring words regarding one's individual duty demand all our admiration: "Better always one's own duty, be it ever so humble, than that of another, however tempting. Even death brings in blessedness itself in the performance of one's own duty; doomed to peril will he be if he performs the duty enjoined on another." (3.35)

Arjuna now has one more question, rather a pertinent one, and that is his last question in this chapter. "Impelled by what, O Krishna, does a man commit sin despite himself?" (3.36) "*Kāma, krodha,*" answers Krishna, "desire and anger—these are the hostile enemies of man." (3.37)

Desire is insatiable. Once desire is born, it knows not how to die. King Yayāti's experience of desire can throw abundant light on us. Let us cite his sublime experience. King Yayāti was one of the illustrious ancestors of the Pāṇḍavas. He was utterly unacquainted with defeat. He was well conversant with the *Śāstras* (scriptures). Immense was his love for his subjects in his realm. Intense was his devotion towards God. Nevertheless, cruel was his fate. His father-in-law, Śukrācārya, the preceptor of the *asuras* (demons), pronounced a fatal curse on him, and he was forced to marry Śarmiṣṭhā in addition to the daughter Devayānī. Śukrācārya cursed Yayāti with premature old age. Needless to say, the curse took an immediate effect. The inimitable pride of Yayāti's manhood was ruthlessly stricken with age. In vain the king cried for forgiveness. However, Śukrācārya calmed down a little. "King," he said, "I am lessening the strength of my curse. If any human being agrees to exchange the beauty and glory of his youth with you, with your body's deplorable state, then you will get back the prime of your own youth."

Yayāti had five sons. He begged of his sons, tempted them with the throne of his kingdom, persuaded them in every possible way to agree to an exchange of life. His first four sons softly and prudently refused. The youngest, the most devoted, Puru, gladly accepted his father's old age. Lo, Yayāti at once was transformed into the prime of his youth. In no time, desire entered into his body and commanded him to enjoy life to the last drop. He fell desperately in love with an *apsarā* (nymph) and spent many years with her. Alas, his insatiable desire could not be quenched by self-indulgence. Never.

At long last he realised the truth. He fondly said to his dearest son Puru: "Son, O son of mine, impossible to quench is sensual desire. It can never be quenched by indulgence any more than fire is extinguished by pouring ghee [clarified butter] into it. To you I return your youth. To you I give my kingdom as promised. Rule the kingdom devotedly and wisely." Yayāti entered again into his old age. Puru regained his youth and ruled the kingdom. The rest of his life Yayāti spent in the forest practising austerities. In due course Yayāti breathed his last there. The soul-bird flew back to its abode of Delight.*

Bernard Shaw's apt remark on desire can be cited to add to the glory of this experience of Yayāti:

> There are two tragedies in life. One is not to get your heart's desire. The other is to get it.
>
> —*Man and Superman*

The role of desire is over. Now let us jump into the fury of anger. Desire unfulfilled gives birth to anger. Anger is the mad elephant in man. To our wide surprise, most of the celebrated Indian sages of the hoary past found it almost impossible to conquer anger. They used to curse human beings in season and out of season, at times, even without rhyme or reason. The sage Durvāsa of the Mahābhārata topped the list of the sages successfully consumed with anger. He was at once austerity incarnate and ire incarnate.

Desire satisfied, life grows into a bed of thorns. Desire conquered, life grows into a bed of roses.

**Rāmāyana* 7.58–59; see also *Viṣṇupurāṇa* IV.10 and *Brahmapurāṇa* 146.11–18.

Desire transformed into aspiration, life flies into the highest liberation, life dines with the supreme salvation.

Knowledge, Action and Sacrifice

In the second and third chapters of the Gita, Sri Krishna blessed Arjuna with a few glimpses of yogic light. In the present chapter, he blesses Arjuna with a flood of spiritual light. He widely and openly reveals the secrets of Yoga. Hard is it for Arjuna to believe that Sri Krishna taught Vivasvān (the Sun-God) this eternal Yoga. Vivasvān offered it to his son Manu, and Manu imparted it to his son Īkṣvāku; from him it was handed down to the royal rishis. Long before Sri Krishna's birth, Vivasvān saw the light of day. Naturally Sri Krishna's declaration would throw Arjuna into the sea of confusion.

The eternal mystery of reincarnation is now being revealed. Says Krishna: "Arjuna, you and I have passed through countless births. I know them all; your memory fails you. Although I am birthless and deathless and the Supreme Lord of all beings, I manifest Myself in the physical universe through My own Maya, keeping My *Prakṛti* [nature] under control." (4.5-6)

Māyā means 'illusion'. It also means the unreality of ephemeral things. The unreality is personified as a female, who is also called Maya. The words 'dharma' and 'maya' are the constant and spontaneous expression of the Indian soul. According to Shankara, the Vedāntin of the Himalayan peak, there is only one Absolute Reality, Brahman, without a second. Advaita or Monism, deriving from Vedānta, is his momentous philosophy. There is only Brahman. Nothing outside Brahman exists. The world as it stands before our mental eye is a cosmic illusion, a deceptive prison. It is only when true knowledge dawns on us that we will be in a position to free ourselves from the meshes of ignorance and from the snares of birth and death.

A thing that is, is real. A thing that appears is unreal. An eternal Life is real. Ignorance and death are unreal. Maya is a kind of power filled with mystery. We know that electricity is a power, but we do not actually know what electricity is. The same truth is applicable to Maya. God uses His Maya-Power in order to enter into the field of manifestation. It is the process of the becoming of the One into many and again the return of the many into the original One.

Prakṛti means 'nature'. It is the material cause as well as the original cause of everything in the manifested creation. *Puruṣa* is the silent Face. *Prakṛti* is the activating Smile. *Puruṣa* is the pure, witnessing consciousness, while *Prakṛti* is the evolving and transforming consciousness. In and through *Prakṛti* is the fulfilment of the Cosmic Play.

Arjuna knew Sri Krishna as his dear cousin; he later knew him as his bosom friend; later still he knew him as his beloved Guru or spiritual Teacher. Here in this chapter he comes to know Sri Krishna as the Supreme Lord of the world. Krishna says, "Whenever unrighteousness is on the ascendent and righteousness is on the decline, I body Myself forth. To protect and preserve the virtuous and put an end to the evil-doers, to establish dharma, I manifest Myself from age to age." From these soul-stirring utterances of Sri Krishna, we immediately come to learn that He is both the ultimate Knowledge and the Power supreme. Confidently and smilingly, He is charging Arjuna with a high-voltage spiritual current from His great Power-House.

Saṃbhavāmi yuge yuge (4.8)

I body Myself forth from age to age.

Sri Krishna now declares himself an Avatar. An Avatar is the direct descent of God. In the world of manifestation, He embodies the Infinite.

In India, there was a spiritual Master who declared himself to be an Avatar. Unfortunately he became an object of merciless ridicule, both in the West and in the East. As he could not put up a brave fight against this biting sarcasm, he finally had to change his unsuccessful policy. His proud statement went one step further: "Not only I, but everybody is an Avatar." Since everybody is an Avatar, who is to criticise whom? Lo, the self-styled Avatar is now heaving a sigh of relief.

It may sound ridiculous, but it is a fact that in India practically every disciple claims his Guru to be an Avatar—the direct descent of God. A flood-tide of enthusiasm sweeps over them when they speak about their Guru. The spiritual giant Swami Vivekananda could not help saying that in East Bengal, India, the Avatars grow like mushrooms. On the other hand, to pronounce that there has been and can be only one Avatar, the Son of God, is equally ridiculous.

Each time an Avatar comes, he plays a different role in the march of evolution according to the necessity of the age. In essence, one Avatar is not different from another. A genuine Avatar, Sri Ramakrishna, revealed the Truth: "He who was Rama, He who was Krishna is now in the form of Ramakrishna."*

There are two eternal opposites: good and evil. According to Sri Krishna, when wickedness reaches the maximum height, God has to don the human cloak in the form of an Avatar. Sri Krishna's advent had to deal with the darkest evil force, Kaṃsa. Similarly Herod, the peerless tyrant, needed the advent of Jesus Christ. The birth of Christ demanded the ex-

---

*See Swami Nikhilananda, *Vivekananda: A Biography,* Calcutta, 1987, p. 67.

tinction of the life of ignorance. *Janmāṣṭamī*, the birth of Krishna, is celebrated throughout the length and breadth of India with a view to leaving the sea of ignorance and entering into the ocean of knowledge.

The easiest and most effective way to conceive of the idea of a personal God is to come into contact with an Avatar and remain under his guidance. To have an Avatar as one's Guru is to find a safe harbour for one's life-boat. In this connection, we can cite Vivekananda's bold statement: "No man can see God but through these human manifestations.... Talk as you may, try as you may, you cannot think of God but as a man."*

According to many, as the Buddha is the most perfect man, so is Krishna the greatest Avatar the world has ever seen.

There are also *Aṁśāvatāras* (partial Avatars). But Sri Krishna is a *Pūrṇāvatāra* (complete Avatar) in whom and through whom the Supreme is manifested fully, unreservedly and integrally. When human aspiration ascends, the divine Compassion descends in the cloak of an Avatar.

"As men approach Me, so do I accept them." (4.11) There can be no greater solace than this to the bleeding heart of humanity. If we accept Krishna with faith, He illumines our doubting mind. If we

---

*Swami Vivekananda, *The Yogas and Other Works,* Swami Nikhilananda, ed., New York, 1953, p. 420.

accept Krishna with love, He purifies our tormenting vital. If we accept Krishna with devotion, He transforms the ignorance-night of our life into the knowledge-sun of His eternal Life.

Sri Krishna now wants our mind to be riveted on caste. He says that it was he who created the fourfold order of the caste system according to the aptitudes and deeds of each caste. There are people who give all importance to birth and heredity and deliberately ignore those who are abundantly blessed with capacities and accomplishments. The result is that society has to suffer the ruthless buffets of stark confusion. True, birth and heredity have their own importance. But this so-called importance cannot offer us even an iota of light and truth. It is by virtue of action, serene and noble, that we grow into the Highest and manifest the Deepest here on earth.

From verse 16 to verse 22 we see Krishna throwing light on action, inaction and wrong action. Action—that is to say, true action—is not just to move our body. Action is self-giving. Action is to abandon attachment. Action is to bring the senses under control. Wrong action is to dance with desire. Wrong action is to disobey one's inner being. Wrong action is to swerve from the path of Truth, esoteric and exoteric.

In common belief inaction is tantamount to inertia, sloth and so forth. But true inaction is to throw oneself into ceaseless activities while keeping the conscious mind in a state of sublime tranquility or trance.

Faith and doubt close the fourth chapter. Faith is not a mere emotional feeling to stick to one's belief. It is a living inner breath to discover, realise and live in the Truth. Faith is the exercise taken by a seeker of his own will to force himself to stay in the all-seeing and all-fulfilling Will of God. The Yajur Veda tells us that consecration blossoms in self-dedication, Grace blossoms in consecration, faith blossoms in Grace and Truth blossoms in faith. What else is faith? To quote Charles Hanson Towne:

> I need not shout my faith. Thrice eloquent
> Are quiet trees and the green listening sod;
> Hushed are the stars, whose power is never
> spent;
> The hills are mute: yet how they speak of
> God!

Doubt is naked stupidity. Doubt is absolute futility. Doubt is outer conflagration. Doubt is inner destruction.

Saṁśayātmā vinaśyati —"The possessor of doubt perishes." (4.40) He is lost, totally lost. To him the path of the Spirit is denied. Also denied is the secret of life's illumination. Says Krishna: "For the doubting man, neither is this world of ours, nor is the world beyond, no, nor even happiness." (4.40)

In *Nyāya* (logic), one of the six systems of Indian philosophy, we notice that doubt is nothing but a conflicting judgment regarding the character of an object. Doubt comes into existence from the very fact of its recognition of properties common to many objects, or of properties not at all common to any objects. Doubt is that very thing which is wanting in the regularity of perception. Also doubt, being non-existent, exists only with non-perception.

Doubt is an all-devouring tiger. Faith is a roaring lion that inspires an aspirant to grow into the all-illumining and all-fulfilling Supreme.

Poor, blind doubt, being quite oblivious of the true truth that faith is the most forceful and most convincing affirmation of life, wants to give a violent jolt to man's life-boat.

The poet's haunting words of truth stir our hearts to their very depths:

> Better a day of faith
> Than a thousand years of doubt!
> Better one mortal hour with Thee
> Than an endless life without.

Renunciation

Comparison was the order of the day. So is it still. Perhaps forever it shall remain so, especially in the field of manifestation. Renunciation and selfless action are now being compared. This is Arjuna's request.

"Both you extol, O Krishna, renunciation and selfless action. Tell me decisively once and for all, which is the better of the two?" (5.1)

Sri Krishna's immediate answer is: "Both lead to the Bliss supreme, but action is easier, action is superior." (5.2)

The divine Teacher makes it clear, however, that renunciation cannot be achieved in the twinkling of an eye, and to achieve the fruit of renunciation without selfless action is next to impossible.

Yoga is action freed from separativity. The awareness of a separate feeling is the death of renunciation. Action done with a feeling of universal oneness is the glorious birth of renunciation.

Two schools. One school teaches the renunciation of any work whatsoever. The other school teaches the performance of action, right action. One school says: "Stop doing anything." The other school says: "Start doing everything." Alas! Since the message of the Gita has not been truly understood in India, that country abounds in both dry ascetics and unlit men of action.

From action, action springs. Action as such can never put an end to action. Action is continuous. Action is perpetual. No matter how hard we work, how long we work, mere action can never show us the Face of the Supreme. He is a true karma yogi who works for the Supreme and for the Supreme alone. Indeed the karma yogi is also the greatest renouncer, for he seeks nothing, rejects nothing. Likes and dislikes to him have equal importance. At his high command are all pairs of opposites. They exist to affirm him, to fulfil him, to crown him with victory, inner and outer.

Krishna's teachings aim at one Goal, the Bliss supreme. Human temperaments are bound to differ. Human beings have varying tendencies and leanings. Such being the case, it is difficult for Arjuna to assess the most immediate and most direct path.

Action and renunciation are identical. Action is the tree. Renunciation is the fruit thereof. One cannot be greater than the other. The tree and the fruit grow in the bosom of Infinity to be loved by Eternity and embraced by Immortality.

Is there any freedom? If so, where is it? There *is* freedom. It lives in our conscious surrender to the

Supreme's Will. Our unreserved surrender is our infallible oneness with the Supreme. Since the Supreme is the infinite Freedom, we, in essence, cannot be otherwise.

It was Marlowe who said:

> It lies not in our power to love or hate,
> For will in us is overruled by fate.

This is true only when our fate is determined by the ego's extremely limited dictates. This deplorable fate of ours undergoes a radical transformation—stark bondage is transformed into boundless freedom—when we, with our ever-mounting aspiration-flame, live in the soul's unlimited and all-powerful will. What we have within and what we see without is the consciousness of the evolving, expanding and radiating freedom. No matter what kind of freedom it gives us, physical or spiritual, this freedom is not just to succeed bondage or even to replace bondage, but to transform the very breath of bondage into freedom's Immortality. And this is freedom, as a world-figure once remarked, without quotation marks.

Service can do many things for us. First of all, we should know that service done in a divine spirit is the greatest opportunity that we have in our possession to kill our pride and vanity and to obliterate the stamp of ego. It is in dedicated service that we see the universal harmony, we grow into the universal consciousness. Our will becomes God's Will. What we call service is nothing but the fulfilment of the divine Will. Here on earth one has the capacity; another has the need. The capacity and the need must go together. Capacity offered, not only is the need fulfilled, but also the capacity is recognised, the capacity is valued. Capacity by itself receives only partial satisfaction. But when capacity and need run abreast, full satisfaction dawns.

"From each according to his abilities, to each according to his needs." In our daily life, this truth is significantly applicable.

God has to occupy one's mind; and in this state of divine concentration, one should serve humanity. At that very hour, service itself becomes the greatest reward. Although meditation and service constitute totally different approaches in the field of spirituality, work and dedicated service are nothing short of pure meditation.

Krishna now tells us about pleasure and pain. "Sense-pleasure ends in pain. Hence sense-pleasure is shunned by the wise. Constant self-control is the real and perpetual happiness." (5.22-23)

Self-control continued, self-mastery dawns. The world-existence and the world-activity are at the command of self-mastery. The easiest way to achieve self-control is to take the path of self-consecration. Self-consecration is always blessed by the soul's illumination. The turbulent forces of our senses must needs bow down to the soul's illumination. He who has the inner illumination knows that his existence on earth is the embodiment of God and his actions are the expressions of God. He feels that he is never the doer; he is a mere instrument.

We now come to learn from the Gita what the body is. "The body is a city within nine gates." (5.13)

To quote Wesley La Violette from "An Immortal Song" (The Bhagavad Gita):

> The body is a city with many gates
> in which the sovereign mind can rest serenely.
> Within that city is the sacred Temple
> of the Spirit, Mind, where there is no desire
> to act, nor any motivating cause,
> yet always the glad willingness
> to follow Duty when it calls. (5.13–14)

It is true that the body has a sacred temple. Equally true is it that the body itself is hallowed. Walt Whitman's powerful assertion is to be gratefully welcomed: "If anything is sacred, the human body is sacred."

Today the body is the insurmountable obstacle. Tomorrow this very body can be and will be the pride of Divinity, for in and through this body God shows the world what He looks like, what He does and what He is.

Towards the end of this chapter, Sri Krishna firmly says that sensuality has to be shunned totally in order for man to live in and possess Divinity fully. The tiger-passions have to be conquered. The aspirant has to concentrate constantly on his Liberator. Indeed, for him alone is the Goal, the salvation unique.

Self-Control

No more hesitation! No more fear! No more confusion! The first verse of the sixth chapter tells Arjuna that a *saṃnyāsī* and a yogi are one. "He who does his duty with no expectation of the fruit of action is at once a *saṃnyāsī (sāṃkhya yogi)* and a yogi *(karma yogi)*." (6.1) Abstention and selfless dynamism are one.

Needless to say, it is renunciation that unites *Saṃnyāsa* and Yoga. This renunciation is the renunciation of desire and the renunciation of expectation. Action, right action, must be done. Action is no bondage. Action is aspiration. Action is realisation. The Gita demands our freedom from the stark bondage of action and not from action. The evil bondage that is our foe is within us and not without us. So also is our divine friend, freedom. It seems that we are at the mercy of our mind. Milton in his *Paradise Lost* speaks of the mind: "It [mind] can make a hell of Heaven or Heaven of hell." A true devotee can easily transcend this deplorable fate. His aspiration and rejection make him one with God's Will. He soulfully sings:

If I ascend to Heaven, Thou art there;
There too, Thou, if I make my bed in hell.

In this chapter Sri Krishna has used the words 'Yoga' and 'yogi' at least thirty times. Here he tells Arjuna for whom Yoga is meant. "Arjuna, Yoga is neither for an epicure, nor for him who does not eat at all, neither for him who sleeps overmuch, nor for him who is endlessly awake."

Self-indulgence and self-mortification are equally undeserving. To a self-indulgent person, the Goal will always remain a far cry. He who follows the philosophy of Cārvāka* lives in the world of indulgence, which is nothing other than frustration. And this frustration is the song of destruction. The philosopher Cārvāka declares:

> The pain of hell lies in the troubles that arise from foes, weapons and diseases, while liberation *(mokṣa)* is death, which is the cessation of life-breath.

On the contrary, liberation is the life-breath of the human soul. And this life-breath was before the

---

*Cārvāka was an ancient Indian philosopher whose views are known only from the polemics and refutations of other schools (mainly Buddhist and Jain). His system, the *Lokāyata,* was the only materialistic system in India in all its long history and never attained to any special importance. Its followers are often characterised as "those who believe the body to be the Self *(dehātmavādinaḥ).*"

birth of creation, is now in creation and is also beyond creation.

We have dealt with self-indulgence. Now let us focus our attention on self-mortification. The Buddha tried self-mortification. And what happened? He came to realise the true truth that self-mortification could never give him what he wanted—illumination. So he gladly adopted the Middle Path, the golden mean. He accepted neither starvation nor indulgence. With this peerless wisdom the Buddha won his Goal.

Arjuna's sterling sincerity speaks not only for him but also for us. Yoga is equanimity. How can the restless mind of a human being be controlled? Unsteady is the mind. Unruly like the wind is the mind. Krishna identifies himself with poor Arjuna's state of development. Krishna's very consolation is another name for illumination.

"O Arjuna, the mind is unsteady, indeed! To curb the mind is not easy. But the mind can be controlled by constant practice and renunciation." (6.35)

What is to be practised? Meditation. What is to be renounced? Ignorance.

Krishna's firm conviction, "Yoga can be attained through practice" (6.36), transforms our golden dream into the all-fulfilling Reality.

Practice is patience. There is no short-cut. "Patience is the virtue of an ass"—so do we hear from the wiseacres. The impatient horse in us or the hungry tiger in us will instantly jump to this grandiose discovery. But the revealing peace in the aspirant and the fulfilling power in the aspirant will clearly and convincingly make him feel that patience is the light of Truth. The light of Truth is indeed the Goal.

A great Indian spiritual figure, on being asked by her disciples as to how many years of strenuous practice had brought her full realisation, burst into roaring laughter. "Practice! My children, what you call practice is nothing other than your personal effort. Now, when I was at your stage, unrealised, I thought and felt that my personal effort was ninety-nine per cent and God's Grace was one per cent, no more than that. But my utter stupidity died the moment self-realisation took birth in me. I then, to my amazement, saw, felt and realised that the Grace of my merciful Lord was ninety-nine per cent and my feeble personal effort was one per cent. Here my story does not come to an end, my children. Finally I realised that that one per cent of mine also was my Supreme Father's unconditional and soulful Concern for me. My children, you feel that God-realisation is a struggling race. It is not true. God-realisation is always a descending Grace."

What we truly need is patience. When impatience assails us we can, however, sing with the poet: "Thou, so far, we grope to grasp Thee." But when our consciousness is surcharged with patience, we can sing in the same breath with the same poet: "Thou, so near, we cannot clasp Thee."

It is not unusual for us to see that sometimes even an earnest seeker fails in the spiritual path. In spite of the fact that he had faith and devotion in ample measure, he fails to complete his journey. This question haunts Arjuna's heart. He says to Krishna: "Though endowed with faith, a man who has failed to subdue his passion and whose mind is wandering away from Yoga (at the time of passing away) and who fails to attain perfection, that is, God-realisation, what fate does he meet with? Does he not meet with destruction like a rent cloud? He is deprived of both God-realisation and world-pleasure. His fate has deluded him in the path of Yoga. He has nowhere to go. He has nothing to stand upon." (6.37-38)

Alas, the inner world does not accept him, the outer world rejects him and condemns him. He is lost, totally lost. If he is successful, both the worlds will embrace him and adore him. If he fails, he becomes an object of ruthless ridicule.

Before Sri Krishna illumines Arjuna's mind, let us bring Einstein into the picture. The immortal scientist declares:

> If my theory of relativity is proven successful, Germany will claim me as a German

and France will declare that I am a citizen of the world. Should my theory prove untrue, France will say that I am a German and Germany will declare that I am a Jew.

To come back to the Teacher and the student, the Teacher illumines his student's mind with the rays of consolation, hope, inspiration and aspiration: "O Arjuna, no fall is there for him either in this world or in the world beyond. The fatal evil destiny is not for him who does good and who strives for self-realisation." (6.40)

The Teacher also says that he who falls from the path of Yoga in this life enters into a blessed and hallowed house in his next life to continue his spiritual journey.

Each human incarnation is but a brief span and it can never determine the end of the soul's eternal journey. None can achieve perfection in one life. Everyone must needs go through hundreds or thousands of incarnations until he attains spiritual perfection.

A devotee always remains in the breath of his sweet Lord. For him there is no true fall, no destruction, no death. How he has apparently failed, or why he has failed, can be only his surface story. His real story is to be found in his ever-cheerful persistence, in his ultimate victory over ignorance, in his absolute oneness with the Supreme. Let us recall the significant utterance made by Jesus: "Martha, I am the Resurrection and the Life; he who believes in Me, though he die, yet shall he live, and whoever lives and believes in Me shall never die. Do you believe this?" Martha said to Jesus: "Yes, Lord, I do believe." (John 11:25-27)

Similarly, with Arjuna, we can in all sincerity and devotion say to Lord Krishna: "O Krishna, the eternal Pilot of our life-boat, we believe in You." We can go one step ahead: "Krishna, You are our eternal journey. You are our transcendental Goal." (cf. 10.12)

Knowledge Illumined

Out of His infinite Bounty, Sri Krishna tells His beloved disciple that He will give him all that He has and all that He is: Infinity and Eternity. He expects only two things from the disciple in return: Yoga and dependence. We may call this dependence devoted surrender, which is the indivisible oneness of the finite with the Infinite. To know Sri Krishna is to know the Knowledge supreme. To realise Sri Krishna is to realise the life of everything in essence.

Manuṣyānām sahasreṣu …

> Among thousands of men, scarcely one strives for spiritual perfection, and of those who strive and succeed, scarcely one knows Me in essence. (7.3)

It seems that the third verse is throwing cold water on the seeker. Krishna's intention is anything but that. Krishna is not only all Wisdom, but also all Compassion. He wants to tell Arjuna what actually takes place in the spiritual marathon race.

Not for him the Knowledge supreme, to be sure, who owns childish curiosity, shallow enthusiasm, weak determination, flickering devotion or conditional surrender. Any of these undivine qualities will, without fail, fail the inner runner.

The sixth and seventh verses describe the relation that exists between Sri Krishna and the universe. "I am the beginning and the end of the universe. I am the Source of creation and I am the place of dissolution. Beyond Me, there is nothing. All this is threaded upon Me as pearls on a string." (7.6-7)

When we concentrate on "All this is woven onto Me like gems into a necklace," we immediately vision the peerless poet Krishna.

Three qualities of nature: *sattva, rajas, tamas*—harmony, activity and inactivity. Sri Krishna says these three qualities are from Him and in Him, but He is not in them.

Sattva is the chief quality of nature. It embodies harmony. Let us know the existence of harmony in relation to the universe. To quote Dryden:

> From harmony, from Heavenly harmony
> This universal Frame began:
> From harmony to harmony
> Through all the compass of the notes it ran,
> The diapason closing full in Man.

The possessor of the sattvic quality has undoubtedly a heart of gold. He knows that his life has a significance of its own. His breath is pure. His patience is luminous. Unparalleled is his fortitude. Infallible is his certainty.

Rajas is the second quality. A man with the rajasic quality is always filled with dynamic passion. He wants to possess the world. He wants to rule the world. He has practically no time to enter into the world of inner illumination. His life cherishes just two things: fight and conquest. He has the possibility either to be a divine warrior or to be a warrior of stark falsehood. He has the strength to build a temple of Truth. He has also the strength to break and destroy it. Unfortunately he often breaks and destroys the temple owing to his unlit vision and the mad elephant in him.

Tamas is the third quality. It is sloth, darkness, ignorance, sin and death. It is also the worldly delusion and the deluding illusion.

Sattva is the soul with clear vision.
Rajas is either the fruitful or fruitless life.
Tamas is the dance of death.

Sattva manifests itself through the aspiring light.
Rajas manifests itself through the desiring might.
Tamas manifests itself through the darkening night.

A man of virtue wants to live the truth.
A man of action wants to enjoy the world.
A man of inactivity enjoys nothing. On the contrary, he is enjoyed constantly by darkness, ignorance and death.

A man of virtue has a friend: aspiration.
A man of activity has a friend: inspiration.
A man of inactivity has a friend: delusion.

A man of virtue tries to live in the truth of the present, past and future.

A man of action wants to live in the glorious present. He does not care much for the future.

A man of inactivity does not live in the proper sense of the term. He sleeps. His days and nights are made of lightless sleep.

The first one wants to transcend himself soulfully. The second one wants to expand himself forcefully. The third one destroys himself unconsciously.

Those who follow the inner path have four distinct roles to play:

Ārta, the depressed, the afflicted. Life is a bed of thorns. He has realised this truth and cries for life's transformation. He wants to possess a bed of roses. Pain is his painful possession. He can successfully sing with Francis Thomson:

> Nothing begins and nothing ends
> That is not paid with moan;
> For we are born in other's pain
> And perish in our own.

Jijñāsu, the seeker, the enquirer. What he wants is knowledge. Knowledge tells us why a man suffers.

Further, since knowledge embodies power, it transforms the breath of suffering into the breath of seeing and kindling knowledge.

Arthārthī, the seeker of true wealth, the Truth absolute. He has no sorrow. He has no earthly desire. He wants to live in perpetual freedom, liberation.

Jñānī, the wise. He who is wise knows that the Supreme is everywhere and the Kingdom of Heaven is within him. He lives in the Supreme. His life is the life of oneness with the Supreme. His world is the world of true fulfilment. Thickest is the intimacy between him and the Supreme. (7.16-17)

Sri Krishna continues: "Noble and good are they all, but I hold the wise, the enlightened as My chosen soul and My own Self; fully united, absolutely one we are. When his life has played its role, when the hour of silence knocks at his door, I place him in My Heart where the Breath of Eternal Life grows." (7.18-19)

The Imperishable Infinite

Brahman is the Imperishable Infinite. Another name for Brahman is Aum. Aum is the Creator. Aum is the creation. Aum is in the creation. Aum is beyond the creation.

This chapter begins with a volley of most significant questions. *Brahman, adhyātma, karma, adhibhūta, adhidaiva, adhiyajña*—what are these? The Lord answers: "The Imperishable Absolute is Brahman. *Adhyātma* is the self-revealing Knowledge of Brahman's primaeval Nature. *Karma* is the birth of activity, natural and normal. *Adhibhūta* is the perishable material manifestation. *Adhidaiva* is the knowledge of the Shining Ones. *Adhiyajña* is the sacrifice made by Me in order to unite the manifestation of finite forms with My infinite Life." (8.3-4)

Krishna affirms that self-realisation or the realisation of Immortality must be achieved during life in the body and nowhere else. As each human being creates limitation, imperfection and bondage, so also is he capable of transcending them. He will finally enter into the planes of fulness, perfection and freedom.

Our existence is the result of a previous existence. This earth of ours is the result of an earth that existed before. Everything is evolving. The essence of evolution is an inner and outer movement. This movement or change takes place even in the world of Brahmā.* Even after attaining Brahmā's world, one cannot escape the snares of rebirth. To be sure, our earthly days and nights are nothing but an infinitesimal second in comparison to the days and nights of Brahmā. A thousand ages breathe in Brahmā's one single day, and a thousand ages breathe in Brahmā's one single night.

No use in taking shelter in our earthly days and nights, for they are fleeting. No use in taking shelter in Brahmā's days and nights either, for they are also not eternal. We can, we should and we must take shelter only in Lord Krishna's eternal Heart, which is our safest haven, where no day is required, no night is required since His Heart is Infinity's Light and Eternity's Life.

Nothing else do we need save devotion. Our choice supreme is devotion. Our heart of devotion

---

*The personal god Brahmā (masculine) is not to be confused with the impersonal Absolute Brahma(n) (neuter). Because of this, many authors use the word Brahmā in the nominative and Brahman in the stem-form (as Sri Chinmoy does in this book), for in this way the two names or principles are distinguishable without exact scholarly transliteration.

responds to His Heart of Love. Says He: "Only the devotion unswerving has the direct and free access to My Life immortal, My Truth absolute." (8.22)

What is within will sooner or later be manifested without. The possessor of divine thoughts will also be the doer of divine deeds. It is possible only for a dedicated and aspiring man to think of God consciously while leaving the earth scene.

Krishna tells us how a yogi enters into the Ultimate after leaving his mortal sheath. "His senses are under control. His mind is placed in the heart. He meditates on Me. Aum he soulfully chants. He gives up *prāṇa*, the life-breath, and enters into the ultimate realisation in Me." (8.12-13)

Madame H. P. Blavatsky, the founder of Theosophy, observed Aum in a very simple and significant way. She said, "Aum means good actions, not merely lip-sound. You must say it in deeds." In order to know what Aum is and what it stands for, one is well advised to study the Upanishads that speak of Aum. The Māṇḍūkya Upanishad offers us the significance of Aum explicitly.

The meaning of Aum can be known from books, but the knowledge of Aum can never be had by studying books. It must be achieved by living an inner life, a life of aspiration, that will transport the aspirant to the higher levels of consciousness. The easiest and most effective way to go up high, higher, highest is to surcharge oneself with pure love and genuine devotion. Doubt, fear, frustration, limitation and imperfection are bound to surrender to devoted love and surrendered devotion. Love and devotion have the power unparalleled to own the world and be owned by the world. Love God's manifestation; you will find that the cosmic creation is yours. Devote yourself to the cause of the cosmic manifestation; you will see that it loves you and claims you as its very own.

It is true that knowledge can give you what love and devotion give, but very often knowledge is not cultivated for the sake of Truth, but for the fulfilment of desires. Fruitless is the pursuit of knowledge when desire looms large in it. When the aspirant is all love and devotion, he soars.

During his journey's flight he sings:

No more my heart shall sob or grieve.
My days and nights dissolve in God's own Light.
Above the toil of life my soul
Is a bird of fire winging the Infinite.

At the end of his journey's flight he sings:

I have known the One and His secret Play
And passed beyond the sea of ignorance-dream.
In tune with Him, I sport and sing.
I own the golden Eye of the Supreme.

He has now grown into his own Goal. Self-amorous he sings:

Drunk deep of Immortality,
I am the root and boughs of a teeming vast.
My Form I have known and realised.
The Supreme and I are one—all we outlast.*

---

*Sri Chinmoy, "Revelation", *My Flute,* New York, 1972.

The Secret Supreme

The secret supreme is the Knowledge supreme. It cannot be told. It has to be realised. This supreme secret is written in letters of gold in the inmost recesses of each divinely human heart. It rejects none, no, not even the one who is dead in sin. He who has no faith in what Krishna says will have no escape from the fetters of ignorance. To have faith is to have a piece of singular good fortune. Like exemplary devotion, faith too needs a personal God, and it has one. Faith is not blind belief. Faith is not a blind, unquestioning surrender to the sacred books. Faith is the conscious awareness of one's limitless freedom.

Krishna says: "O Arjuna, salvation is not for him who has no faith. Forever he is bound to the sorrows of life and to the pangs of death." (9.3) He who walks along the road of faith will see for himself the Truth supreme here on earth. The determination of the seeker's aspiring heart is his mystic faith. The conviction of the seeker's revealing soul is his triumphant faith. An ordinary, unaspiring man is buoyed by the worlds of false hopes. But a man of faith always lives in the worlds of forceful affirmation. Cheerfully and unreservedly he heaps more and more fuel of sterling faith at the altar of God. Needless to say, the flowering of his soul runs apace.

Krishna smilingly says: "The deluded slight Me, My human incarnations, knowing not that I am the Lord Supreme of all beings." (9.11)

To recognise an Avatar is not an easy thing. Either one has to be blessed by the Avatar himself or one has to possess the gift of inner vision. An aspirant has to prepare himself in order to recognise an Avatar. He has to shun sense-pleasure. He must not be controlled by passions. It is he who has to control his passions. He has to breathe in constantly the breath of purity. Fear he has to tear down. Doubt he has to smite. Peace he has to invoke. Joy he has to imbibe.

To perform abstruse rites and ceremonies is not necessary. Self-giving is the only thing required. He accepts everything with greatest joy. We can start our inner journey offering Him leaves, flowers and fruits. Even the smallest act of offering to God is the truest step on the path of self-discovery and God-discovery. We think. If we offer our 'thinking' to God, this very act of offering our thought will ultimately make us one with God the Thought. An ordinary man feels that he thinks just because he lives. But Descartes holds an altogether different view: "I think, therefore I am." This "I am" is not only the fruit of creation, but also the breath of creation. Significant are the words of Bertrand Russell: "Men fear thought as they fear nothing else on earth—more than ruin, more even than death."

If we can discover a true, divine thought, then in no time God will ask or compel time to be on our side. Nothing save time can help us feel the breath of Truth and touch the Feet of God. We can own Eternity's Time if we truly want to. Sweet and meaningful are the words of Austin Dobson: "Time goes, you say! Ah no! Alas, Time stays, *we* go."

We serve. If we serve Him, Him alone in humanity, we become one with His absolute Reality and His universal Oneness. We must not forget that our dedicated service must be rendered with a flood-tide of purest enthusiasm.

Verse 29 is a very familiar and popular one. "To Me all are alike, I know no favour. I know no disfavour. My loving devotees who worship Me are in Me. I am also in them." (9.29) This is an experience that stands out in bold relief in a true seeker's life. There is no special privilege. Everybody is granted the same opportunity. It goes without saying that a true devotee has already gone through arduous spiritual disciplines. Now if he grows into a genuine devotee and becomes dear and intimate to Krishna, then it should be understood that he is getting the result of his past iron disciplines and severe austerities. No pain, no gain. No sincerity, no success. Have aspiration. It will accelerate your progress, inner and outer.

The devotee aspires. Sri Krishna resides in his aspiration. The devotee realises. In his realisation he discovers that Krishna is his eternal breath. A devotee is never alone. He has discovered the true truth that his self-sacrifice unites him with his Lord. The more he consciously offers himself to the Lord, the stronger becomes their divine bond of union, nay, oneness.

Anityam (not lasting, fleeting); *asukham* (pleasureless, joyless).* The outer world abides in our earth-bound consciousness. This earth-bound consciousness can be transformed into the Eternal Consciousness through aspiration, devotion and surrender. The Eternal Consciousness houses perpetual joy. Liberation has to be achieved here in this world. Any man of promise will gladly subscribe to Emerson's dauntless declaration: "Other world! There is no other world. Here or nowhere is the whole fact."

When we look at the world with our inner eye, the world is beautiful. This beauty is the reflection of our own divinity. God the Beautiful has our as-

---

*The author here refers to verse 9.33 of the Bhagavad Gita, in which both of these words are used and whose second line reads, "You who have come into this transient *(anityam)* and joyless *(asukham)* world, devote yourself to Me."

piring heart as His eternal Throne. We, the seekers of the Supreme, can never see eye to eye with Nietzsche's proud philosophy. He utters: "The world is beautiful, but has a disease called man." On the contrary, we can say in unmistakable terms that the world is beautiful because it has been illumined by a supernal beauty called man.

Anityam and *asukham* cannot blight the heart of a true seeker. His faith is married to his golden fate. He sings and sings:

> My eternal days are found in speeding time;
> I play upon His Flute of rhapsody.
> Impossible deeds no more impossible seem;
> In birth-chains now shines Immortality.*

---

*Sri Chinmoy, "Immortality", *My Flute*, New York, 1972.

The Perfection Divine and Universal

What is within us is perfection. What is without us is imperfection. The outer world can have perfection only when the inner world inspires, guides, moulds and shapes the outer world.

Yesterday dreamt of today as perfection. Today dreams of tomorrow as perfection. Perfection already achieved pales into insignificant imperfection before the birth of the fast approaching future.

Perfection grows. It has been doing so since the beginning of the creation's birth. Unlike us, God has one Dream: perfect Perfection. This perfect Perfection must shine in the aspiring hearts of individuality and universality so that the absolute Reality can be the total expression of the Cosmic Vision.

Everybody is dear to God. But the sweetest and the most intimate relation exists only between a devotee and the Lord. A true devotee worships the Lord with no desire's brood. The Lord blesses him not only unreservedly but also unconditionally. What a devotee needs is the determined strength of his heart. Once he has achieved it, his self-realisation will no longer remain a far cry.

To understand the Truth is one thing. To believe in it is another. Not to understand the Truth is no crime, far from it. But to disbelieve the Truth is nothing short of an unpardonable sin. A child does not understand his father's vast wisdom. Nevertheless, his faith in his father's wisdom is spontaneous and genuine.

Sri Krishna is the wisdom absolute. He is the glory supreme. His glory nobody understands. No, not even the gods. Arjuna may not understand Krishna, but his implicit faith in Krishna speaks for him: "O Krishna, You are the Lord of the Lords. Supreme are You. This I believe. Neither the gods nor the demons comprehend Your mysterious manifestations. The source of all beings are You. You are known by Yourself alone." (10.12-15)

> If the thing believed is incredible, it is also incredible that the incredible should have been so believed.
>
> —*St. Augustine*

Belief is the complete liberty of the mind. Belief is the full independence of the heart.

Krishna now makes it clear to Arjuna that his divine glory can be elucidated and demonstrated but can never be exhausted. The universe in its entirety is but a tiny spark of his infinite magnitude.

Pāṇḍavānām Dhanañjayaḥ, says Krishna. "Among the Pāṇḍavas I am Dhanañjaya." (10.37) Dhanañjaya is an epithet of Arjuna. Each person has one body, one mind, one heart and one soul. How can one standing in front of another say that he is verily the other person! Does it not sound absurd? It does so only when we live in the physical, not when we live in the oneness of the Spirit.

When we declare that all human beings are one and the same, we just state a bare fact that we inwardly believe or try to believe. It is the sense of identification that makes us one. Krishna says: "I am this, I am that, I am everything." Again He says that He is the best, highest and mightiest in everything. Does it mean that His Consciousness is tinged with preference? Does He discriminate? No, He has no preference, He has no discrimination. "Arjuna, I am the Self seated in the heart of all beings. I am the beginning and middle and also the end of all beings." (10.20)

Krishna wants to illumine Arjuna's mind by saying that in the process of cosmic evolution He is unveiling and manifesting His own Perfection. His divine manifestations are endless. He has mentioned only a few by way of example. From Him spring permanence, goodness and mightiness. He tells Arjuna that he has not to learn His divine manifestations in minute detail. It will simply confuse his mind. "I established the whole universe with a portion of Myself." (10.42) Knowing this, the seeker in Arjuna can easily satisfy his hunger.

"I am the seed of all things, animate or inanimate." (10.39) Arjuna now realises that Krishna is not the mere body. He is the Self all-pervading. Arjuna wishes to know under what particular form the Self is to be worshipped. "Under all forms," is Krishna's immediate reply. Nothing there is without the Self. The Self is in all and all is in the Self. This is the wisdom that the seeker's knowledge must possess.

The Gita teaches us the purest oneness. This oneness is the inner oneness. This inner oneness is at once spontaneous and unique. This oneness can never be truncated or dwarfed by the mind. The realm of oneness is far beyond the approach of the physical mind.

Self-knowledge is the knowledge of universal oneness. Divine perfection can be founded only on the fertile soil of universal oneness. Serve humanity precisely because Divinity looms large in humanity. Know Divinity and you will in no time realise God's Immortality in you and your Immortality in God. God in man and man in God can only announce the truest embodiments of perfect Perfection.

The Vision of the Universal Form and the Cosmic Manifestation of the Lord

Out of His infinite Bounty, boundless Love and deepest, soulful Concern, Sri Krishna has unveiled the secret supreme that He is in everything and He embodies everything. Arjuna's stark delusion has been removed and dispersed. He now enjoys his soul's translucent peace.

Sri Krishna speaks out of the abundance of His Love. Arjuna listens to Him with his heart's loftiest devotion and believes in Him unreservedly and soulfully. Arjuna's singular belief cries for its transformation; his aspiration cries for an experience. His mind understands the Truth. But his heart pines to vision the Truth and to live the Truth. Hence he needs this experience, unavoidable and inevitable. Sri Krishna graciously and immediately grants it, the experience unparalleled.

"O Arjuna, behold in My Body the entire universe." (11.7) Arjuna's physical eyes naturally fail to vision it. The Lord grants him the eye of supernal vision, the eye that sees the unseen—the yogic eye.

The body that the Lord speaks of is a spiritual body. Hence to see the spiritual body, Arjuna must needs be endowed with a spiritual eye. The body signifies form. The formless abides in this form. The Vision Transcendental and the Reality Absolute play in unison in and through the cosmic form. The body of flesh and blood undergoes innumerable vicissitudes, but not the body of unlimited, divine form and deathless substance. This divine body is the embodiment and revelation of Truth's Divinity, Infinity, Eternity and Immortality.

Sañjaya says to Dhṛtarāṣṭra, "O King, Krishna, the supreme Master of Yoga, the Almighty Lord, reveals to Arjuna His Form divine, supreme. Arjuna now sees Krishna as the Supreme Godhead, Parameśvara." (11.9)

Arjuna sees the many in the One Supreme possessing myriad mouths, numberless eyes, limitless marvels, wielding divine weapons, wearing divine garments and jewels, bearing celestial garlands of supernal fragrance. The effulgence of a thousand suns bursting forth all at once in the skies will hardly equal the supreme splendour of the Lord. Arjuna beholds Infinity in multiplicity, in the divine person of Krishna. Overwhelmed, ecstasy flooding his inmost being, with his hands folded, his head bowed, he exclaims, "O Lord, in You, in Your body, I behold all gods and all grades of beings, with distinctive marks. I see even Brahmā seated resplendent on

His lotus-throne and seers and sages all around, and symbolical serpents—all divine." (11.15)

When we go up with all our heart's snow-white flaming aspiration, we enter into the Cosmic Consciousness of the seers. This path is an upward path. It is the path of embodiment and realisation. There is another path known as the path of revelation and manifestation. This path is the downward path. Here our consciousness flows down through the cosmic energy, the symbolic serpents, circling and spiralling.

Verses 15 to 31 eloquently and psychically describe what Arjuna saw in Krishna with his newly acquired yogic sight.

The fight is yet to start. The mighty warriors are ready and eager to fight. To his greatest surprise, Arjuna sees the lives of the warriors utterly extinguished in Krishna. Even before the birth of the fight, he sees the death of the warriors. Destroyed they are. As he sees the fires of Krishna's flaming and all-devouring mouth, his very life-breath quivers. The disciple cries out, "Your Compassion, my Lord Supreme, I implore. I know You not. Who are You?" (11.31)

"Time am I. Time, the mighty destroyer, am I. Doomed they are. Whether you fight or not they are already dead. Even without you, your foes will escape no death. Arise, O Arjuna, arise! Victory's glory and renown you win. Conquer your enemies. Enjoy the vast kingdom, enjoy. By Me is ordained their lives' surrendered hush. You be the outer cause. Just be My instrument, nothing more." (11.32–33) *Nimittamātraṃ bhava.* "Be a mere instrument." (11.33b)

There can be no greater pride, no better achievement, than to be God's own instrument, for to be an instrument of God is to be infallibly accepted as His very own. In and through the instrument-disciple, the Master-Guru sees and fulfils God's divine Purpose.

Krishna is the all-devouring Time. This vision, according to our outer eyes and understanding, is terrible. But according to our inner vision and inner comprehension, it is natural and inevitable. Sri Aurobindo says:

> Time represents itself to human effort as an enemy or a friend, as a resistance, a medium or an instrument. But always it is really the instrument of the soul. Time is a field of circumstances and forces meeting and working out a resultant progression whose course it measures. To the ego it is a tyrant or a resistance, to the Divine an instrument. Therefore, while our effort is personal, time appears as a resistance, for it presents to us all the obstruction of the forces that conflict with our own. When the divine working and the personal are combined in our con-

> sciousness, it appears as a medium and condition. When the two become one, it appears as a servant and instrument.*

Krishna Prem, the great seeker, says:

> It is impossible to state in words this wondrous insight. All things remain the same yet all are changed. Time flashes bodily into Eternity; the streaming Flux itself is the Eternal, which, though It moves unceasingly, moves not at all.**

The Upanishadic lore echoes and re-echoes in our aspiring hearts: "That moves and yet That moves not. That is far distant and yet That is close and near." (*Īśopaniṣad* 5)

Time houses Truth. Sri Krishna tells the Truth, the Truth eternal, about Himself. Here we can recollect the significant words of Virginia Woolf, "If you do not tell the truth about yourself, you cannot tell it about other people." Conversely, if you know the spiritual truth about yourself, you must needs know the truth about others. Sri Krishna showed the divine Truth that was Himself.

---

*Sri Aurobindo, *The Synthesis of Yoga,* 4th ed., Pondicherry, 1970, p. 61f.

**Sri Krishna Prem, *The Yoga of the Bhagavad Gita,* London, 1951, p. 107.

We can also cheerfully walk with Marcus Aurelius: "I cannot comprehend how any man can want anything but the Truth."

To doubt the spiritual Master before one's own illumination dawns is not uncommon in the spiritual history of the world. Even some of the dearest disciples of great spiritual Masters have done so. But for the seeker to leave the Master precisely because doubt haunts him is an act of sheer stupidity. Stick, stick unto the last. The blighted doubts will disappear into thin air. The splendour of Infinity and Eternity will blossom in the bosom of time. Your mounting aspiration will accomplish this task.

Arjuna's throbbing heart voices forth, "Thou art the primeval Soul." (11.38a) He cries for Krishna's forgiveness. Owing to his past ignorance, he had not realised Krishna in His divine nature. His past was full of wrong deeds, with ignorance and with carelessness. He begs with a throbbing heart for forgiveness for his acts of omission and commission rendered to Sri Krishna.

"Bear with me as father with his son, as friend with his friend, as lover with his beloved." (11.44a) Sri Krishna no doubt forgives Arjuna. He assumes his normal, natural and familiar form.

Arjuna comes to realise that it is only the Grace divine that has endowed him with the yogic eye to see the Unseen, the Glory supreme of the Lord, the present, past and future.

He also learns from the Lord that "neither the study of the Vedas, nor sacrifice, nor alms, neither austerity nor study can win this cosmic vision." (11.53) Even the gods yearn for a glimpse of this Universal Form which He has just shown to Arjuna out of His boundless compassion.

Faith, devotion, surrender. Lo! Krishna is won. No other way Him to realise, Him to possess.

The Path of Devotion

Arjuna is exceedingly happy and extremely fortunate that he has had the most rare vision of the Cosmic Form. How is it possible for him to be burdened with further philosophical and spiritual questions? The reason is that his vision of the Cosmic Form does not imply that he has reached the Goal of goals. The vision has to be transformed into a living, constant reality in Arjuna's life, and then he has to live in the reality itself. The experience of the vision is good. The realisation of the vision is better. The embodiment of the vision is best. Better than even the best is the revelation of the vision. Finally it is the manifestation of the vision which is divinely and supremely unparalleled.

The path of meditation and the path of devotion are now being compared. Arjuna wishes to learn from Sri Krishna about the two paths: the path of meditation that leads to the Unmanifest and the path of devotion that leads to the personal God—which is the better of the two? Krishna's answer is that each path, devotedly and faithfully followed, leads to the

Goal. But the path of meditation is more difficult and more arduous. The physical body binds us to the material world. Hence it is difficult for us to meditate on the Unthinkable, the Unimaginable and the Transcendental. But if we approach the Lord who assumes human form and who plays His divine Game in the field of His manifestation, our success will undoubtedly be easier, quicker and more convincing, to a degree which our physical minds would not believe possible.

A genuine seeker must dissolve all that he has—ignorance and knowledge—and all that he is—ego and aspiration—in God. Indeed it is most difficult but not impossible. Lo! He is given the golden opportunity to accept the easiest and the most effective path. In this unique path, he has just to offer the fruits of his action to the Lord and he has to dedicate himself—body, mind, heart and soul—to the Lord.

The path of meditation and the path of devotion will lead ultimately to the same goal. Now what makes the aspirant feel that the path of meditation is extremely difficult to follow? The answer is very simple. The aspirant cannot focus his mind's attention on the Unmanifest Beyond; whereas if the aspirant is devoted to the Lord in His manifested creation, and if he wants to see and worship his Beloved in each being, his path becomes undoubtedly easier. Love the form first; then from the form, go to the Formless Beyond. The disciple at the beginning must approach the divinely physical aspect of the Guru and then he has to go beyond, far beyond the Guru's physical form and physical substance in order to commune with and stay in the ineffable and the ever-transcending Beyond.

The disciple wants the easiest path. Sri Krishna kindly consents. He says that the path of meditation is difficult, the path of selfless service is difficult and the path inspired by love and devotion is difficult. But still there is one more path which is extremely easy to follow. In this path, one has merely to renounce the fruit of action. If we cannot do our work as a dedicated service to God, we should not succumb to dark disappointment. We can just work, work for ourselves. We need only offer the fruits of our work to the Lord. However we will do well if we do only that particular work which we feel from within to be right. Naturally we will do the work that is demanded of us by our soulful duty. If we do our soulful duty and offer the fruits to the Lord, in no time our Inner Pilot is won.

The Field and the Knower of the Field

Devotion is more than enough to realise Lord Krishna, the Truth eternal. However, in this chapter Sri Krishna wants to widen Arjuna's knowledge, philosophically and intellectually. Those who harbour philosophical and intellectual questions with regard to the Truth will now truly be satisifed.

We try to avoid and ignore that which creates problems in our life. According to Krishna, this so-called wisdom of ours is nothing short of ignorance. True, we shall not create problems on our own. But if problems do appear, then we have to face them, enter into them and finally conquer them dauntlessly and totally.

Arjuna has already been blessed by the Lord with the inner heights. Now the Lord wants to illumine him with the knowledge of the cosmos wherein he has to play a conscious role.

Matter and spirit. *Prakṛti* and *Puruṣa*. The field and the knower of the field. The body is the field. The soul is the knower thereof. True wisdom lies in realising the Knower Supreme and the cosmos, known and revealed.

There are twenty-four *tattvas*, principles, that go to form the field. The first group of great elements or bases is earth, water, fire, air and ether. The field also houses the ego and the earth-bound mind, the intellect; the five organs of action—hands, feet, tongue and the two organs of elimination; also the sense organs—nose, mouth, eyes, ears, and so on. The five spheres of the senses are sight, smell, taste, hearing and touch.

Only one thing is to be known. To know that the Lord is within the cosmos, without the cosmos and beyond the cosmos is to know everything.

Matter and Spirit (*Prakṛti* and *Puruṣa*) are beginningless. Matter is the primordial substance. Matter is ever-changing. Spirit is always static. Matter is the possessor of infinite qualities. Spirit sees and sanctions. Matter does, grows and becomes. Spirit is consciousness. Spirit is the witness. Matter is the creativity infinite. Spirit is the Reality in man. Spirit is the perceiver of matter. He who has realised Spirit's eternal silence and matter's cosmic dance may live in any walk of life, whether as a doctor or a philosopher, a poet or a singer; he has achieved the perfection of supreme realisation. There are some who realise the Supreme Spirit in meditation; others by knowledge (the *Sāṃkhya* philosophy). There are also others who realise the Supreme Spirit by the yoga of action and selfless service. In addition, there are those who are not aware of it, but who have heard of the Supreme Spirit from others and who have started worshipping it in devotion, and cling firmly to the Truth. They also pass on beyond mortality and cross beyond the snares of death.

Spirit is in matter. It tastes the qualities born of matter. It does experience the physical existence. The qualities acquired determine its rebirth. Spirit is the Supreme Himself. Although Master of the body, it experiences mortal life.

The way to God is to see the Eternal Life in the fleeting life, to know that *Prakṛti*, not *Puruṣa*, is to action attached. All activities, says the Gita, divine and undivine, arise in *Prakṛti*. *Puruṣa* is actionless. No action is possible in *Puruṣa*, for *Puruṣa* transcends both time and space. Yet without *Puruṣa*, there can be no universe, no manifestation.

Spirit is self-existent and all-pervading, whether within the body or without the body; always unaffected the Spirit remains.

To know that *Puruṣa* and *Prakṛti* are one and inseparable is to know the Truth, the Truth of unity and divinity in humanity, which will eventually be manifested as the divinity of humanity.

The Gita does not house arid, logical metaphysics. Its teachings have no need for any support from intellectual argument. Human reason cannot knock at the door of Transcendental Reality. Never. What is the Gita, if not the Transcendental Reality supremely and divinely embodied?

Each human being has to learn five supreme secrets from the Gita:

See the Truth.
Feel the Truth.
Be the Truth.
Reveal the Truth.
Manifest the Truth.

In this chapter we observe that the Gita is at once the significance of life and the divine interpretation of life. Unfortunately, this particular chapter has become the victim of dire contradiction in spite of the very fact that the Gita, from its journey's start to its journey's close, sees not the face of contradiction. The Gita sees and reveals only the face of Truth's unity in multiplicity. Scholars and commentators are at war with each other over their theories. Nor have the philosophers the inclination to shun this battle. Each is inspired to impose his lofty theories on the others. But a genuine seeker of the supreme Truth is truly wise. He prays to the Lord Krishna to have the Gita as his personal experience. Sri Krishna smiles. The devotee cries out:

Thou that hast given so much to me,
Give one thing more, a grateful heart.
Not thankful when it pleaseth me,
As if Thy Blessings had spare days;

> But such a heart, whose pulse may be
> Thy praise.
>
> —*George Herbert*

Lo, the devotee has won the race! The devotee needs a Guru, a Master. Sri Krishna is the Guru and Arjuna is the disciple. An eminent Indian scholar, Hari Prasad Shastri, writes:

> Is the Guru, or Master, an absolute necessity to the realisation of Truth? The reply, according to the Gita, is "Yes." The Guru is the person who teaches the unity of the soul with the Absolute and who lives the life of Sattva. He can be of either sex and, according to the Gita, need not be a recluse, living in the snows of the Himalayas, cut off from the world, speaking through chosen apostles only, and sending fantastic letters through the "astral mail." The Guru of the Gita is a man like any other good man, whom anyone can see at any convenient time, who lives in human society and does not claim any superiority over others.

Finally the Gita tells us that the Guru of all Gurus, the real Guru, is God.

The Three Gunas

Sattva is purity. *Sattva* is light. *Sattva* is wisdom. Happiness and *sattva* stay together. Harmony and *sattva* breathe together. The senses in *sattva* are surcharged with the light of knowledge. If one leaves the body when *sattva* prevails, then to the pure abode of the sages he goes.

Rajas is passion. *Rajas* is desire. *Rajas* is unlit activity. *Rajas* binds the body to action. *Rajas* stays either with stark dynamism or with blind aggression. Restlessness and *rajas* breathe together. To separate toil from *rajas* is practically impossible. *Rajas* is another name for passionate movement. If one dies when *rajas* prevails, then he is reborn among those attached to action.

Tamas is slumber. *Tamas* is darkness. *Tamas* is ignorance. Stagnation and *tamas* stay together. Futility and *tamas* breathe together. Impossible for *tamas* to be separated from naked pangs. *Tamas* is another name for slow death. Death in *tamas* is followed by rebirth among the senseless fools.

Sattva-tree bears the fruit called harmony.
Rajas-tree bears the fruit called pain.
Tamas-tree bears the fruit called ignorance.

Sattva offers to the world at large luminous knowledge; *rajas,* passionate greed; *tamas,* rank delusion. He whose life is flooded with *sattva* looks up into the skies. Hence he goes to higher spheres. He whose life is fired with *rajas* looks haughtily around the world. Hence here he dwells. Blind is he whose life is covered with tenebrous *tamas*. Stone blind is he. Hence down he sinks.

The Lord says that he who understands the origin of action in these three-fold qualities of *Prakṛti,* and at the same time understands *Puruṣa,* who is beyond the qualities, comes to Him and enters into His Nature. Finally, when he goes beyond the length and breadth of these three qualities—*sattva, rajas* and *tamas*—he drinks deep the Nectar of Immortality. (14.19–20)

> Do all the good you can,
> By all the means you can,
> In all the ways you can,
> In all the places you can,
> At all the times you can,
> To all the people you can,
> As long as ever you can.
>
> —*John Wesley*

This precisely is expected of a sattvic man. Now you may ask, how is it that he too has to transcend his nature? Is he not unique in his service to mankind? He may be unique in his large human family, but perfect freedom he has yet to achieve. Silently, secretly and, alas, at times even unconsciously the poor sattvic man is attached to the fruits of his generous service, to the effects of his sublime knowledge. So with a view to achieving absolute freedom and perfect perfection, a sattvic man has to transform and transcend his nature.

After having transcended the three *gunas,* one has to make a choice whether one wants to remain in the Transcendent, far above the field of manifestation, or one wants to serve the eternal Breath of the Infinite in humanity and inspire humanity to the realisation of the supreme bliss, peace and power.

Not one, not two, but three significant questions Arjuna asks. What are the marks of one who has transcended the three qualities? How does he behave? How does he go beyond the three qualities? (14.21)

Krishna's answers are:

The yogi who has transcended the three qualities in his own life will neither hate nor crave for the fruits of *sattva, rajas* or *tamas.* Within and without he is flooded with his soul's equanimity. He is absolutely independent. He has realised the absolute independence of his divinity within. Something more: he serves God with his sterling devotion. He does it soulfully. He serves mankind with all his love. He does it unconditionally. He sees God and God alone in all human souls. Such a yogi ultimately becomes without fail the Self Supreme. (14.22-26)

The Supreme Puruṣa

Chapter XIII has taught us the truth that there is a field and there is a Knower of that field. Chapter XIV has thrown abundant light on the field, the Cosmic Play of *Prakṛti*. In this particular chapter we shall learn about the Knower, the Self Universal and the Self Supreme.

This chapter begins with a tree. This tree is called the world-tree. Unlike earthly or botanical trees, this tree has its root above in the Supreme. The Supreme is its only Source. Downward are its branches spread. The Vedas are its leaves. He who has fathomed the depths of the ever-changing and ever-evolving world has all the Vedic knowledge at his disposal.

Here on earth this tree is not free. It is caught by its own action and reaction here in this world of ours. It is fondly nourished by the three qualities of *Prakṛti*. If one wants to discover the beginning, the end and the very existence of this tree, then one has to free himself totally from this temptation-tree.

A tree signifies aspiration. This aspiration ultimately rises up to the Highest. Countless are the

Indian *sādhus* (monks) who sit under the trees and enter into the world of deep meditation. The aspiration of the tree inspires them and arouses their dormant aspiration. Lord Buddha had his enlightenment at the foot of the Bodhi Tree. The world knows it.

The Gita is an ocean of spirituality. Spirituality's most affectionate daughter is poetry. The subtle breath of poetry is always fondled by life-energising spirituality. Let us identify our consciousness with the consciousness of a poet when he speaks of a tree.

> Poems are made by fools like me,
> But only God can make a tree.
>
> —*Joyce Kilmer*

Since poetry is my forte, I gladly take the liberty of seeing eye to eye with the blessed poet.

To come back to our philosophical tree, the wise cut down its root with the axe of detachment. This is the way to liberation. This is the way to the supreme good.

A wise man lives in perfect self-control. He is devoted to the Truth unreservedly and unconditionally. He wants God and God alone, Who is the fount of the world within, the world without and also the world beyond. The happenings, encouraging or discouraging, pleasant or unpleasant, divine or undivine, do not stir his mind, not to speak of his inner existence. He swims in the sea of fruitful silence and equanimity. Being the master of the senses, he lords it over them. He comes to Krishna, his only haven. No sun, no moon, no fire are necessary in His Abode. This Abode is the Source of the entire universe. It is all illumination. From His eternal Abode there is no return.

It is not for the deluded but for the seers who are endowed with divine vision to recognise or understand Him, the Lord Supreme, Who enters into the body, resides in the body and experiences the qualities of nature and leaves the body at His chosen Hour.

To be sure, all serious efforts of a man will be of no avail until he has achieved steadiness in his mind, until his outer nature is at his command, until his heart overflows with love and devotion to his spiritual Teacher (Guru), until he serves the living Breath of the Lord in humanity.

There are two aspects of creation: the perishable and the imperishable. Beyond these two is the Impersonal Supreme. This Impersonal Supreme is at once all-pervading and all-sustaining.

The Lord says: "I, the *Puruṣottama*, the Supreme Being, transcend both the perishable and the imperishable." (15.18)

There are four Vedas. All four Vedas significantly speak of this Supreme Being.

> The Being Supreme, thousand-headed,
> thousand-eyed, thousand-footed;

He pervades the length and breadth of
the earth.
He is beyond all ten corners.
(*Ṛgveda* X.90.1–2)

Here 'thousand' undoubtedly means infinite. Infinity is manifesting itself through the finite in the field of manifestation.

Puruṣottama is beyond formlessness and form, beyond impersonality and personality. In Him the mightiest dynamic urge and the profoundest silence stay together. To Him, they are one. To Him are one, Heavenly freedom and earthly necessity, the ever-changing form of the earth and the changeless Reality infinite.

Forces Divine and Forces Undivine

The world, fear and bondage enjoy the deepest intimacy. He who thinks of God is ultimately loved by the world. He who loves God has no fear. Bondage he transcends.

He who feels that sense-pleasure and the supreme joy are one and the same is utterly mistaken. Self-indulgence and the Goal of life never can and never will meet.

To see God one has to be practical, absolutely practical, both in the world of realisation and in the world of manifestation. Nobody can be more practical than one who is endowed with spiritual qualities. His life is guided, protected and illumined by the forces divine.

Fear fears to stay with him who has perfect faith in God. His heart is purity. His mind is freedom. Duplicity? He knows not what it is. His love he uses to love mankind. He expects love in return only if so is the Will of God. His service he offers to the Supreme in humanity, having utterly destroyed the root of expectation, nay, temptation-tree with the sharp axe of his wisdom-light. Devotion's delight and meditation's silence constantly breathe in him. Violence is too weak to enter into his fort of thought, word and deed. Purest sincerity he has. Mightiest self-sacrifice he is. He wears no man-made crown, but a God-made crown which God Himself cherishes. The name of this divine crown is humility.

He who is devoured by the undivine forces is not only unspiritual but impractical in the purest sense of the term. Never can he stay alone even if he wants to. Vanity, anger, ostentation and ego arouse him from his slumber and compel him to dance with them. Secretly but speedily ignorance comes and joins them in their dance, and then cheerfully and triumphantly it teaches them the dance of destruction.

His ego he uses to buy the world. His anger he uses to weaken and punish the world. His vanity and ostentation he uses to win the world. Consciously he offers himself to the glorification of sense-pleasure. Alas, he himself fails to count his imaginary projects, for they are countless, innumerable. What he has absolutely as his own is his self-praise. What he infallibly is, is verily the same.

He says to charity and philanthropy: "Look, I am sending you two to the world. Remember, I am not giving you to the world. Bring back from the world for me name and fame. Come back soon!" Charity and philanthropy humbly listen to his command.

They go running toward the world. They touch the world. They feed the world. They forget not to bring back name and fame from the world for their master. The master receives his coveted prize: name and fame. Alas, to his utter astonishment, futility follows his name and fame.

His life is the hyphen between sin and hell. What is sin? Sin is the taste of imperfect ignorance. What is hell? Hell is the ruthless torture of unsatisfied desires and the fond embrace of ignorance fulfilled.

At first the seeker has to take ignorance and knowledge separately. Later on he realises that in both ignorance and knowledge 'That' exists. Let us kindle our aspiration-flame with the soulful lore of the Īśā Upanishad.

Avidyayā mṛtyuṃ tīrtvā . . . (*Īśopaniṣad* 11)

By ignorance he crosses beyond death;
by knowledge, Immortality he enjoys.

The chapter comes to its close with the word *śāstras* (scriptures). *Śāstras* are not to be ridiculed. *Śāstras* are the outer attainments of the inner experiences and realisations of the seers of the Truth. The goal supreme is not for those who look down upon the spiritual experiences and realisations of the seers of the hoary past. They are committing a Himalayan blunder if they feel, on the strength of their vital impulses, that they can practise meditation and learn the secrets of inner discipline unaided. Personal guidance is imperative.

Easy to say: "I follow my own path." Easier to deceive oneself. Easiest to starve one's inner divinity that wants to reveal and manifest itself.

The Teacher enjoins the student: "O my Arjuna, follow the *śāstras*." (cf. 16.24)

The Threefold Faith

The outer man is what his inner faith is. All our activities, physical, vital and mental, have a common fount. The name of that fount is faith. With our faith we can create, control, conquer and transform our fate. To be sure, what we unconsciously call human faith is nothing short of the divine Will in us and for us.

What does a sattvic man do with his luminous faith? He uses his faith to invoke and worship the Supreme. What does a rajasic man do with his passionate faith? He uses it to worship and satisfy the deities. What does a tamasic man do with his tenebrous faith? He worships the unsatisfied, dissatisfied, hungry, obscure, impure and earth-bound spirits and ghosts.

They say that in the West, food has very little to do with faith. In India the link between food and faith is almost inseparable. Our Upanishadic seers cried out: *Annaṃ brahma*—"Food is the Brahman." (*Taittirīyopaniṣad* III.2)

A sattvic man eats the foods that are fresh, pure and soothing so that he can acquire energy, health, cheerfulness and a long life. Sour, salty and excessively hot foods are liked by a rajasic man. Illness captures him. Pain tortures him. A tamasic man also has to eat after all. He avidly eats the foods that are stale, tasteless, impure and filthy. The result of his eating can be better felt than described.

Austerity does not mean physical torture, far from it. Mortification of the flesh only a devilish nature can enjoy. God the Merciful does not demand our physical torture. He wants us to have the soulful light of wisdom—nothing more and nothing less. Austerity means a dedicated body, a pure mind, a loving heart and an awakened soul. The outer austerity grows in the fertile soil of simplicity, sincerity and purity. The inner austerity grows in the fecund soil of serenity, tranquility and equanimity. Sattvic austerity wishes no reward. Gain, honour and fame, rajasic austerity expects and demands. Self-immolation or the destruction of others, tamasic austerity wants and cherishes.

A seeker of the transcendental Truth and sex-forces can never run abreast. The seeker walking along the path of self-discovery and God-discovery must know what true celibacy is. To quote Krishna Prem:

> A neurotic celibacy with the so-called unconscious mind full of thwarted sex, issuing in a welter of more or less disguised fan-

> tasy, is the very worst condition to be in for one who seeks the inner life. Such a condition may, like extreme bodily weakness, give rise to strange experiences and visions, but it will quite effectively prevent any real treading of the Path. Sex will be transcended; it cannot be suppressed...with impunity.*

The chapter ends most soulfully with the Brahman. Brahman is divinely designated by the three soul-stirring words: *Aum tat sat.* (17.23)

Aum is the mystical symbol supreme. Aum is the real name of God. In the cosmic manifestation is Aum. Beyond the manifestation, farthest beyond is Aum.

Tat means 'That', the Nameless Eternal. Above all attributes, majestic 'That' stands.

Sat means Reality, the Truth infinite.

We have to chant *Aum* and then begin to perform our life's divine duties.

We have to chant *Tat* and then offer to humanity all our achievements, energising and fulfilling.

We have to chant *Sat* and then offer to God what we inwardly and outwardly are, our very existence.

---

*Sri Krishna Prem, *The Yoga of the Bhagavad Gita,* London, 1951, p. 173.

Abstention and Renunciation

Slowly, steadily and successfully we are now climbing up the last rung of the Gita-ladder. Here we shall almost have the quintessence of the entire Song.

Arjuna wishes to learn the nature of abstaining from action, the nature of renouncing the results of action and also the difference between these two.

The Lord tells him that *saṃnyāsa* is abstention from desire-prompted action. *Tyāga* is the renunciation of the fruits of action.

Saṃnyāsa and *sāṃkhya yoga* are identical, while *tyāga* and *karma yoga* are identical.

To our widest surprise, even now in India there is a blind belief that a realised soul does not work, cannot work or even is not supposed to work on the physical plane. Alas, the poor realised soul has to cut off his existence from the activities of the world! If such is the case, then I believe that self-realisation is nothing short of severe punishment, an undesirable achievement, loaded with the heavy weight of futile frustration.

To be sure, a realised person is he who has liberated himself from the snares of stark bondage. If he does not work with his body, mind, heart and soul in the world, for the world, and if he does not help seekers on the Path, then who else is competent to lead the struggling, crying and aspiring humanity to its destined Goal?

For liberation, renunciation is essential. Renunciation does not mean the extinction of the physical body, the senses and the human consciousness. Renunciation does not mean that one has to be millions of miles away from world activities. Renunciation does not say that the world is a fool's paradise. True renunciation not only breathes in this world, but divinely fulfils the life of the world.

The Īśā Upanishad has taught us: "Enjoy through renunciation." (*Īśopaniṣad* 1) Let us try it. Unmistakably we will succeed.

Right action is good. Desireless action is verily the best. This dedication is called the true *tyāga*.

Some spiritual teachers hold that action is an unnecessary evil, that it leads man to perpetual bondage. They violently and proudly assert that all action, with no exception, must be ruthlessly shunned. Sri Krishna graciously illumines their folly. He says that *yajña* (sacrifice), *dāna* (self-giving) and *tapas* (self-discipline) must not be shunned, for *yajña*, *dāna* and *tapas* are the true purifiers. Needless to say, even these actions must be performed without the slightest attachment.

Renunciation of duty to humanity is never an act of spiritual realisation or even an act of spiritual awakening. The bliss of freedom is not for him who forsakes duty for fear of bodily displeasure and mental suffering. His false and absurd anticipation will undoubtedly lead him to the world of ignorance, where he will be compelled to dine with fear, anxiety and despair.

He is a man of true renunciation who neither hates a disagreeable action when duty demands it, nor is eager to perform only good and agreeable action.

The Lord says: "To renounce all action completely is not possible for an embodied soul. He who renounces the fruit of action is the true renouncer." (18.11)

When desire is totally rejected and personal gain is sincerely not wanted by a seeker, then only perfect freedom shines within and without him.

The Gita is the revelation of spirituality. Sooner or later all must take to spirituality. There need not and cannot be any compulsion. To force others to accept the spiritual life is an act of stupendous ignorance. A real Guru knows that his is not the role of a commander-in-chief. He never orders even his dearest disciples. He just awakens and illumines their consciousness so that they can see the Truth, feel the Truth, follow the Truth and finally become the Truth.

In numerous ways Sri Krishna has imparted the most inspiring wisdom to Arjuna. At the end He says: "Arjuna, having reflected on wisdom fully, do as you like." (18.63)

Something more Sri Krishna has to say: "Arjuna, My supreme Word, My inmost secret of all, I tell you. To you I unfold My Heart's secret, for dear to Me you always are. Offer your love to Me. Devote yourself to Me. Bow to Me. Give Me your heart. You will without fail come to Me. This I promise you. Arjuna, you are dear to Me. Surrender all earthly duties to Me. Seek your sole haven in Me. Fear not, grieve not, I shall liberate you from all sins." (18.64-66)*

Truth is to be offered only to the earnest seekers. Sri Krishna sweetly cautions Arjuna that the Truth that Arjuna has learned from Him is not to be offered to a man with no faith, no devotion and no self-discipline. No, not for him Sri Krishna's supreme Truth, whose life is tinged with mockery and blasphemy.

Now Sri Krishna wants to know if Arjuna has understood Him, His revelation. He also wants to know if Arjuna is freed from the grip of delusion and the snares of ignorance.

---

*Verse 18.66 of the Bhagavad Gita (here beginning with "surrender all...") is one of the three essential mantras or teachings of the Śrīvaiṣṇavas (Viśiṣṭādvaita school). It is called the *caramaśloka,* the 'supreme verse'.

"Krishna, my sole Saviour, gone is my delusion. Destroyed is my illusion. Wisdom I have received. Your Grace has done it, Your Grace supreme. Firmly do I stand freed from doubts. My doubts are no more. I am at Your command. Your command I implore. I am ready. I shall act." (18.73)

The human soul has gloriously succeeded in emptying all his ignorance-night into the Transcendental Soul of eternal Light. The Transcendental Soul has triumphantly sung the song of Infinity, Eternity and Immortality in the aspiring heart of the human consciousness.

Victory, victory to the crying and bleeding heart of the finite. Victory, victory to the Compassion-Flood and the Illumination-Sky of the Infinite.

Victory of the world within glows! Victory of the world without grows!

Victory achieved. Victory realised. Victory revealed. Victory manifested.

ABOUT SRI CHINMOY

Sri Chinmoy is a fully realised spiritual Master dedicated to inspiring and serving those seeking a deeper meaning in life. Through his teaching of meditation, his music, art and writings, his athletics and his own life of dedicated service to humanity, he tries to offer ways of finding inner peace and fulfilment.

Born in Bengal in 1931, Sri Chinmoy entered an ashram (spiritual community) at the age of 12. His life of intense spiritual practice included meditating for up to 14 hours a day, together with writing poetry, essays and devotional songs, doing selfless service and practising athletics. While still in his early teens, he had many profound inner experiences and attained spiritual realisation. He remained in the ashram for 20 years, deepening and expanding his realisation, and in 1964 came to New York City to share his inner wealth with sincere seekers.

Today, Sri Chinmoy serves as a spiritual guide to disciples in centres around the world. He advocates "the path of the heart" as the simplest way to make rapid spiritual progress. By meditating on the spiritual heart, he teaches, the seeker can discover his own inner treasures of peace, joy, light and love. The role of a spiritual Master, according to Sri

Chinmoy, is to help seekers live so that these inner riches can illumine their lives. He instructs his disciples in the inner life and elevates their consciousness not only beyond their expectation, but even beyond their imagination. In return he asks his students to meditate regularly and to try to nurture the inner qualities he helps them bring to the fore.

Sri Chinmoy teaches that love is the most direct way for a seeker to approach the Supreme. When a child feels love for his father, it does not matter how great the father is in the world's eye; through his love the child feels only his oneness with his father and his father's possessions. This same approach, applied to the Supreme, permits the seeker to feel that the Supreme and His own Eternity, Infinity and Immortality are the seeker's own. This philosophy of love, Sri Chinmoy feels, expresses the deepest bond between man and God, who are aspects of the same unified consciousness. In the life-game, man fulfils himself in the Supreme by realising that God is his own highest Self. The Supreme reveals Himself through man, who serves as His instrument for world transformation and perfection.

In the traditional Indian fashion, Sri Chinmoy does not charge a fee for his spiritual guidance, nor does he charge for his frequent concerts or public meditations. His only fee, he says, is the seeker's sincere inner cry. He takes a personal interest in each of his students, and when he accepts a disciple, he takes full responsibility for that individual's inner progress. In New York, Sri Chinmoy meditates in person with his disciples several times a week and offers a regular Friday evening meditation session for the general public. Students living outside New York see Sri Chinmoy during worldwide gatherings that take place three times a year, during visits to New York or during their Master's frequent trips to their cities. They find that the inner bond between Master and disciple transcends physical separation.

Sri Chinmoy accepts students at all levels of spiritual development, from beginners to advanced seekers, and lovingly guides them inwardly and outwardly according to their individual needs.

Sri Chinmoy personally leads an active life, demonstrating most vividly that spirituality is not an escape from the world, but a means of transforming it. He has written over 1,100 books, which include plays, poems, stories, essays, commentaries and answers to questions on spirituality. He has painted thousands of mystical paintings, and his drawings of "soul-birds" number in the millions. He has also composed thousands of devotional songs. Performing his own musical compositions on a wide variety of instruments, he has offered a series of several hundred Peace Concerts in cities around the world.

A naturally gifted athlete and a firm believer in the spiritual benefits of physical fitness, Sri Chinmoy encourages his students to participate in sports. Under his inspirational guidance, the international Sri Chinmoy Marathon Team organises hundreds of road races, including the longest certified race in the world (1,300 miles), and stages a biennial global relay run for peace. Sri Chinmoy has also taken up weightlifting and achieved phenomenal feats of strength, to demonstrate that inner peace gained through meditation can be a tangible source of outer strength.

For more information about Sri Chinmoy, to learn how to become his student, or to attend free meditation classes at a Sri Chinmoy Centre near you, please contact:

Aum Publications
86-10 Parsons Blvd.
Jamaica, NY 11432

OTHER BOOKS BY SRI CHINMOY

Meditation:
Man-Perfection in God-Satisfaction

Presented with the simplicity and clarity that have become the hallmark of Sri Chinmoy's writings, this book is easily one of the most comprehensive guides to meditation available.

Topics include: Proven meditation techniques that anyone can learn • How to still the restless mind • Developing the power of concentration • Carrying peace with you always • Awakening the heart centre to discover the power of your soul • The significance of prayer. Plus a special section in which Sri Chinmoy answers questions on a wide range of experiences often encountered in meditation. $9.95

Beyond Within:
A Philosophy for the Inner Life

"How can I carry on the responsibilities of life and grow inwardly to find spiritual fulfilment?"

When your simple yearning to know the purpose of your life and feel the reality of God has you swimming against the tide, then the wisdom and guidance of a spiritual Master who has crossed these waters is priceless. Sri Chinmoy offers profound insight into humanity's relationship with God, and sound advice on how to integrate the highest spiritual aspirations into daily life.

Topics include: The spiritual journey • The transformation and perfection of the body • The psyche • Meditation • The relationship between the mind and physical illness • Using the soul's will to conquer life's problems • How you can throw away guilt • Overcoming the fear of failure • The purpose of pain and suffering • Becoming conscious of your own divine nature • and more. $13.95

My Life's Soul-Journey: Daily Meditations for Ever-Increasing Spiritual Fulfilment

In this volume of daily meditations, Sri Chinmoy offers inspiring thoughts and practical guidelines for those who seek a life of ever-increasing inner fulfilment. In these pages, the simple yet powerful language of the heart rings clear with the message of love, compassion, inner peace and oneness with the world and all its people. Each day's offering resonates with the innate goodness of humanity and encourages the reader to bring this goodness to the fore. $13.95

Death and Reincarnation

This deeply moving book has brought consolation and understanding to countless people faced with the loss of a loved one or fear of their own mortality. Sri Chinmoy explains the secrets of death, the afterlife and reincarnation. $7.95

Kundalini: The Mother-Power

En route to his own spiritual realisation, Sri Chinmoy attained mastery over the Kundalini and occult powers. In this book he explains techniques for awakening the Kundalini and the chakras. He warns of the dangers and pitfalls to be avoided, and discusses some of the occult powers that come with the opening of the chakras. $7.95

Yoga and the Spiritual Life

Specifically tailored for Western readers, this book offers rare insight into the philosophy of Yoga and Eastern mysticism. It offers novices as well as advanced seekers a deep understanding of the spiritual side of life. Of particular interest is the section on the soul and the inner life. $8.95

The Summits of God-Life: Samadhi and Siddhi

A genuine account of the world beyond time and space, this is Sri Chinmoy's firsthand account of states of consciousness that only a handful of Masters have ever experienced. Not a theoretical or philosophical book, but a vivid and detailed description of the farthest possibilities of human consciousness. $6.95

Inner and Outer Peace

A powerful yet simple approach for establishing peace in your own life and the world.

Sri Chinmoy speaks of the higher truths that energise the quest for world peace, giving contemporary expression to the relationship between our personal search for inner peace and the world's search for outer peace. He reveals truths which lift the peace of the world above purely political and historical considerations, contributing his spiritual understanding to the cause of world peace. $7.95

Eastern Light for the Western Mind
Sri Chinmoy's University Talks

In the summer of 1970, in the midst of the social and political upheavals that were sweeping college campuses, Sri Chinmoy embarked on a university lecture tour offering the message of peace and hope embodied in Eastern philosophy. Speaking in a state of deep meditation, he filled the audience with a peace and serenity many had never before experienced. They found his words, as a faculty member later put it, "to be living seeds of spirituality." These moments are faithfully captured in this volume of 42 talks. $6.95

A Child's Heart and a Child's Dream
Growing Up with Spiritual Wisdom—
A Guide for Parents and Children
Sri Chinmoy offers practical advice on a subject that is not only an idealist's dream but every concerned parent's lifeline: fostering your child's spiritual life, watching him or her grow up with a love of God and a heart of self-giving.
Topics include: Ensuring your child's spiritual growth • Education and spirituality—their meeting ground • Answers to children's questions about God • A simple guide to meditation and a special section of children's stories guaranteed to delight and inspire. $7.95

The Master and the Disciple
What is a Guru? There are running gurus, diet gurus and even stock market gurus. But to those in search of spiritual enlightenment, the Guru is not merely an 'expert'; he is the way to their self-realisation. Sri Chinmoy says in his definitive book on the Guru-

disciple relationship: "The most important thing a Guru does for his spiritual children is to make them aware of something vast and infinite within themselves, which is nothing other than God Himself."

Topics include: How to find a Guru • How to tell a real spiritual Master from a false one • How to recognise your own Guru • Making the most spiritual progress while under the guidance of a spiritual Master • What it means when a Guru takes on your karma • Plus a special section of stories and plays illustrating the more subtle aspects of the subject.

$7.95

Everest-Aspiration

These inspired talks by one who has reached the pinnacle are invaluable guideposts for others who also want to go upward to the highest, forward to the farthest and inward to the deepest.

Topics include: Dream and Reality • Satisfaction • Imagination • Intuition • Realisation $9.95

Siddhartha Becomes the Buddha

Who exactly was the Buddha? In ten dramatic scenes, Sri Chinmoy answers this question from the deepest spiritual point of view. The combination of profound insight and simplicity of language makes this book an excellent choice for anyone, young or old, seeking to understand one of the world's most influential spiritual figures. $6.95